Yankee Journal

Harold Putnam

Early years in Boston
Boston Latin School
Dartmouth College
Journalist – Boston Globe
Massachusetts Legislature
Three Speakers of the House
Interracial marriage
Presidential appointment

All rights reserved

Copyright © 1998 The Putnam Family Trust

No part of this publication may be reproduced, stored in a retrieval system, or transmitted in any form or by any means whatsoever, whether electronic, mechanical, magnetic recording, or photocopying, without the prior written approval of the Copyright holder, excepting brief quotations for inclusion in book reviews.

First printing March 1998

ISBN: 1-57502-762-3
Library of Congress Catalog Card Number: 98-91329

If this book is not available at your bookstore, please use coupon on last page.

Author addresses:
P.O. Box 3821
Vero Beach, Florida, 32964
Fax: 561-231-0195
eMail: hputnam@compuserve.com

Manufactured in the United States of America

3212 East Highway 30 • Kearney, NE 68847 • 1-800-650-7888

Other Books by the same Author

Dartmouth Book of Winter Sports, Editor

Skating - with Dwight Parkinson

Voice of Reason

The Putnams of Salem Village

Dedicated

to the Baker Library of Dartmouth College
and the libraries of the world -
custodians of everything we know

"Books are the carriers of civilization. Without books, history is silent, literature dumb, science crippled, thought and speculation at a standstill.

"Without books, the development of civilization would have been impossible. They are the engines of change, windows on the world, lighthouses in the sea of time."

Barbara W. Tuchman, American historian
Quoted in the Authors League Bulletin, November 1979

Chronology of the Author

1916 -   Born at 65 Arlington Street in the Hyde Park section of
             Boston. The son of Harold Barnes Putnam and Martha
             Hyde (Sargent) Putnam - a 12th generation descendant of
             John Putnam who arrived at Salem in the Massachusetts
             Bay Colony in 1640.

1933 -   Graduated from Boston Latin School, the oldest public
             school in America.

1937 -   Graduated from Dartmouth College in Hanover,
             New Hampshire.

1938 -   Became a reporter for The Boston Globe

1943-1946 - Lieutenant, j.g., USNR, serving in all theatres of
             World War 2.

1948 -   Elected to the Massachusetts House of Representatives,
             the 59th member of the Putnam family to serve in "The
             Great and General Court of Massachusetts."

1951 -   Selected one of the first ten "Greater Boston Young Men
             of the Year" - along with John F. Kennedy and
             Edward W. Brooke.

1953 -   Graduated from Boston University Law School.

1954 -   Admitted to the Massachusetts Bar.

1956 &1958 - Ran for Congress.

1957 -   Admitted to the Florida Bar.

1958 -   Went to Washington as Legislative Counsel to the late
             U.S. Senator Leverett Saltonstall.

1963 -   Became Administrative Assistant to Speaker
             Joseph W. Martin, Jr. at the Capitol.

1970 -   Appointed New England Regional Director of the
             U.S. Department of Health, Education and Welfare by
             President Nixon.

1980 -   Married Marlene Putnam, noted oil painter, and moved
             to Florida to practice law and write.

TABLE OF CONTENTS

Chapter

Chapter 1

THE EARLY YEARS

Hyde Park was a good place to be born in 1916. Although it was in the process of being absorbed by the City of Boston, it still had all the characteristics of a small town.

Our streets were lined with large trees, usually maples and elms, and many streets were named after trees. Mine was Elm Street. The trees shaded the neighborhood and beckoned us to the nearby woods.

An estate farm, dating back at least one hundred years to the settling of the town, lay on the south slope of Grew's Woods, north of the Hazelwood railroad station – reachable through an urine-scented underpass. We played baseball on a stony field there and searched the woods for flower and tree specimens for our school projects.

"Let's go down to Grew's" was an invitation to adventure in the days of my youth. You could skate on the brook in the winter and fall in. I did once, and walked home freezing to death.

You could play baseball on the stony field, and risk getting a bad hop that might strike you in the nose. Or you could roam through unspoiled woods, whose days were obviously numbered by the population growth of the adjacent big city.

"Play around the house" my mother was apt to instruct me. She felt more comfortable if I were within sight, rather than a half mile away. Few cars used either Elm Street or Arlington Street in the 1920s, and the public streets were more essential to boys than to drivers – or at least we thought so.

I guess you could call the eastern portion of Hyde Park, where I lived, a middle-class WASP neighborhood. Almost all of the families were of English origin and the Protestant faith. Many, as I learned later about myself, were direct descendants of the original settlers of the Massachusetts Bay Colony. Nason, Barnes, Chittick, Parker, Smith, House and Noyes are names that will ring bells in the consciousness of anyone familiar with colonial history.

On Arlington Street, the Nason, Chittick and Parker families housed pretty girls of my own age. Lucy Chittick became a school teacher and her younger sister, Ruth, accompanied me through grade school from the kindergarten on. I remember Ruth for three things – she was very smart. She usually wore some homemade shorts under her dress – quite different from the apparel of other girls.

But most embarrassing was the performance of my dog, Rex, on the Chittick lawn. Rex was a particularly horny male dog, and his feats became notorious throughout our neighborhood. One day a playmate next door yelled at me: "Come on. We gotta get Rex."

Where was Rex? Fornicating vigorously on the front lawn of the Chittick property. Not only fornicating, but stuck so that he could not get free. Half the neighborhood were fascinated spectators.

"Rex, come on home," I demanded. He was monumentally uninterested. He was beyond giving any thought to where his next meal was coming from. Someone suggested that we spray the pair with water. That worked.

Ruth never mentioned that scene upon her lawn. My recollection is that she was not home at the time of the big event. There was never a dull moment when Rex was around.

I found Rex under my Christmas tree in 1925. I think I still believed that Santa Claus, in his great wisdom, had deposited him there. Not until later did I ask: "Where'd you get him?"

"Angell Memorial Hospital in Boston." Later when I went to Boston Latin School I had to walk right by it, and I learned that it was probably the first veterinary medicine facility for pets in the United States. Their first-rate dog pound nurtured Rex. I hope they would have been as proud of his achievements as I was.

The achievements were not all sexual. Some of them were almost acrobatic. My father used to let him ride on the running board of his car – always from home to his store a mile away, but once as far as Cape Cod. Rex could even put his front paws up on the front fender, and still hang on. Pedestrians used to stop and watch as Rex went by.

Two households contained boys my own age. One was the home of Russell DeMerit, probably our only non-WASP neighbor. Sounds French. Russ acquired the nickname "Fat" and he earned it by being about 50 percent fatter than the rest of us. He and I managed to excel at football by combining our assets into an unbeatable trick offense. We would fake a run through the line by Fat, while I took the ball around an end. And then we would fake an end run, and hand the ball to Fat to plunge through the line. Nobody wanted to volunteer to stop Fat, when he managed to get up full speed.

Thinking back over those days, I am struck by the fact that those families had some characteristics that are less common today. None of the parents had drinking problems, and none ever heard of harmful drugs. Every family had both a father and a mother living together. They were all Protestant and all church-going. All the fathers worked and all the mothers stayed at home caring for the kids.

Not until much later did I pursue the origin of my own family. Even writing a book about it – The Putnams of Salem Village. Twelve generations back, in 1640, John Putnam was one of the original settlers of Salem Village (now Danvers, Massachusetts). He came from Aston Abbotts in Buckinghamshire County, England, near Puttenham in Hartfordshire. "Putnam" dates back at least to the Domesday Book of 1086 – William the Conqueror's first census of England.

Even before that the Romans had occupied the land north of London and east of Oxford. Some of their coins are still being found in what were formerly Putnam farmlands. The legions of Rome were in those parts for about four hundred years after the death of Christ.

In fact, the name of the family village – Puttenham – which is now and probably then was pronounced Putnam – seems to have been derived from the Latin word Puteus. It means a deep well. Puttenham seems to indicate "a village around a deep well."

My male line in America produced John (1579 - 1662) and his son Thomas (1614 - 1696). Thomas produced Joseph, (1669 - 1725) who was elected at age 22 to bring an end to the witchcraft hysteria in 1692. And Joseph fathered Israel, (1718 - 1790). Israel wound up as second in command to General George Washington in the American Revolution.

Israel was born in the family homestead, which was built in 1648. Three hundred and fifty years old in 1998. Until 1991, it was the oldest house in America still owned by the original family. The farm/estate is now divided by Route 1 in Danvers, Massachusetts.

Israel was the fourth generation; I am the twelfth. My branch went to Sutton, Massachusetts, before the Revolutionary War. Sutton is southeast of Worcester and in the heart of what was once prime Indian country.

After the Revolution, they migrated to the White River Valley of Vermont, after epidemics and wars had ended the opposition of the Abenaki Indians. One hundred acre land grants were available, some of them including rich farm land on the flood plains along the river and its upper tributaries.

My grandfather, Willard Cushing Putnam, one of ten children, came back to Massachusetts around the 1880s, and my father, Harold Barnes Putnam, was born in Milton, Massachusetts, in 1891.

When I came along in 1916, I was named for my father – a common Puritan practice! – and called Junior. I was never particularly fond of that name and fortunately I eventually outgrew it. Put – pronounced like a golf putt – was more to my liking. That nickname dated back at least to the American Revolution – the General was called Old Put. It persisted until my college classmates came up with Hal.

My father (1891–1979), lived with his grandparents, Warren and Lucinda (Ross) Barnes, at 27 Elm Street, through his young manhood and many years of his marriage Mr. and Mrs. Barnes constructed the house around the turn of the century. John Barnes, a likely ancestor, was a general merchant in the Plymouth Colony in the early 1630s.

Dad was next door to Gilbert Lincoln Sargent (1861–1932) and Nellie (Wilcox) Sargent at number 25 Elm Street, and had the good sense to marry the third of their four daughters, Martha Hyde Sargent. The Sargents probably connect back to William Sargent, one of the first settlers of Newbury on the Merrimac River in the 1630s. I was born at 65 Arlington Street, only two houses away, and the family moved into 27 Elm Street around 1918, when I was two years old. My father and mother, and then my sister, occupied it until 1997 – almost a century in the same family.

One of the nicest things about the early days was that doctors made house calls. Dr. John A. Morgan made a house call at 65 Arlington Street on the afternoon of February 15, 1916 to deliver me! And my baby book indicates that he was sociable enough to linger with the family after the delivery and to sign my baby book on the proper line.

Doctors were readily available for childhood diseases. Dr. Bennett would arrive speedily upon call during my early years, and was available at his office for minor bumps and injuries. He was a roly-poly guy with fat jowls that jiggled while he talked and joked good-naturedly.

He would waddle into our house, carrying a large black

bag full of magic pills that usually did the job for which he intended them. He was not only our "doc" – he was a family friend.

At least I thought of him as my friend until he arrived one day upon some mission relating to me – when I felt 100% healthy. My mother had requested some medical service that seemed to involve me.

"Let's go upstairs to a bedroom," he suggested, and he and my mother led the way to her bedroom.

"Take your pants off," he directed, "and then you can lie back on mother's bed." Only then did I begin to feel some alarm. My feet dangled over the edge of the bed, and my "teapot" – the most secret part of my body – was fully exposed. Teapot was what old Yankees called the male organ in those days.

"This won't hurt very much, and it will soon be over," he tried to soothe me – with the worst fib anyone ever told me! He proceeded with no anesthesia!

The next thing I knew I felt a white-hot searing pain at the tip of my penis – a pain that diminished only very slowly over the course of at least a week. And I gradually became aware that my prick would never be the same. I thought it had been growing very nicely, and never understood why some people think that they can improve upon the blessing that nature conferred upon us males.

My mother tried an explanation that appears in my baby book: "Age 5 1/2, circumcised... Not necessary, but from preference." Whose preference?

My mother was twenty-two when she was married, and twenty-seven when this violation occurred. My father was circumcised, so I doubt very much that my mother had ever seen an uncircumcised penis. How could she make an informed judgment? How could she impose a preference when she had no basis for comparison?

My mother entered all my medical milestones on a page in the Baby Book headed: Red Letter Days. How appropriate. The circumcision was certainly a red letter day for me.

It is pertinent that circumcision today is still the most common surgical procedure in the United States – but nowhere else! Only about five per cent of our M.D.'s are willing to perform this malpractice. And such luminaries as Dr. Benjamin Spock, former Surgeon General C. Everett Koop and the American Academy of Pediatrics have opposed it – yet it lingers on.

I hope that the mothers of today can reach a more informed preference than my mother did. While my organ has performed nobly throughout my long life, I can still look down upon it and wish the maternal preference had gone the other way!

Chapter 2

THE CHANGING NEIGHBORHOOD

As my boyhood progressed beyond the circumcision, I became aware of my surroundings. Immigration and the motor vehicle were beginning to change my quiet Yankee neighborhood. An Italian family named Ficcichie moved next door – into a fine house vacated by a family name Butler. Consternation!

"Guineas next door," my father proclaimed. He always had a curt word for folks who were different from Protestant Yankees. Jews, Catholics and Guineas were high on his list of folks in disfavor.

Our shock eased when we learned that the Ficcichies were Baptists, and when diminutive Joie became a smash hit as the leader of the student orchestra at the Hilton School. Johnny, who was my age, became my good friend.

"Let's rig a messenger service between our rooms," he suggested. His bedroom backed up to mine – only about one hundred feet apart. We installed a pulley on each window sill, cut an old bicycle tire into a six inch message container, and then connected everything with a strong line. I think we also rigged a little bell that would dingle-dangle when we had some message to deliver.

The Ficcichie parents spoke mostly Italian, but the several boys were bilingual. Johnny would occasionally regress to Italian – mostly in relationship to girls. The only word I remember is "chamfickee." I still do not know what it means or how to spell it. My good friend Johnny went on to become a medical doctor.

The second invasion of what Boston Mayor James M. Curley called "the newer races" was not so easy to take. Mr. and Mrs. Civitarese moved in across the street – recently off the boat and not well acquainted with the American language and customs. Their troubles began when they called their first child Billie and a year or so later named their second child Willie.

"How's anyone supposed to know the difference between Billie and Willie?" my father complained. A few years later, my uncle intervened when he thought Billie or Willie was being smacked around a little more than was proper in a Puritan family.

Mr. Civitarese went off to his factory job daily on a bicycle, leaving Mrs. Civitarese to deal with the boisterous boys of the neighborhood. Our favorite playground was a stretch of Arlington Street in front of her house, and her telephone line over the street was essential to the kicking and passing game we had invented for the football season.

You had to kick or pass the football over the wire, and try to give it enough distance or clever placing so that the opponent could not catch it. If the ball did not go over the wire, it did not count. If it went over, giving the opponent enough time to catch it, it was one point for the kicker/passer if no catch was made.

I don't think we invited Fat DeMerit to this game. He was not sufficiently agile. But I used to play with Charlie Cass and Bill Black. Bill later became the director of a vast school-building program in Massachusetts. His parents were of Scotch ancestry, and for awhile they housed the Burness brothers – who may have been the first professional soccer players in America.

Everyone except Mrs. Civitarese loved our street game. We became such good punters that I still think the punting is the weakest part of the professional game. In my youth, we kicked better than some pros do today!

In the 1920s, motor vehicles rarely interrupted our street games – maybe one car every fifteen minutes or so. Mrs. Civitarese was our only problem. She would come out of her front door screaming.

"You get outta there... You breaka my telephone... You bad boys." I am not sure that her English was that good at that point in her American life, but we got the point.

"Let's quit until she calms down," Bill or Charlie was apt to say. But we had no intention of giving up entirely. We did not believe that we had injured her telephone line – even though our football did hit it occasionally. We never really gave up playing.

Automobiles were getting more numerous though. The families no longer kept a horse and wagon, as they did before World War I, and the barns behind the houses were available for boys to play in and for the new cars when they arrived. In the mid-1920s, our barn still had a horse stall and the fragrance of a horse still permeated the space. I was told that he was an ex-racehorse, and that he never liked to be beaten. He was in the right family!

The niftiest of the new cars was an electric car Mr. Jeffords purchased. He was the business manager of the Boston Symphony Orchestra, and our best claim to being an upper middle-class neighborhood. We never got to know him very well, because he had no children to play with and didn't seem to have a wife – so we were never able to finagle a ride in his electric car.

"Geez! What's that?" we exclaimed when it first moved effortlessly down Elm Street. No horse to pull it. No throbbing engine. And no gasoline fumes. It seemed to be propelled by some humming magic.

But it ran well and reliably. Not very fast – true – but it seemed to get him around town in classy style. I remember the car so well that I could draw a picture of it today. The memory makes me wonder why the auto industry is having such difficulty seventy years later manufacturing an electric car. The idea is not all that new, and the reality is not all that new either!

I have a vague memory of white horses racing down nearby River Street, pulling a steaming fire apparatus, but the Fire Department was motorizing after World War I. Horse-drawn wagons came by occasionally – the rag man and the street cleaning crew – and Mr. Ferris blessed them. He was a little old guy whose backyard backed up to ours. We could look over our wooden fence, and observe the development of the best garden in town.

If a horse could contain himself no longer and dumped horse buns onto Arlington Street, Mr. Ferris was out there posthaste to scoop them up and save them for his backyard garden. We had discovered the reason for his superior horticulture.

My dad ran a motorcycle shop at 40 Fairmount Avenue – phone number Hyde Park 0808. In those days, you picked up the phone and spoke the number to a nice lady named Celia Shreenan. She personally connected the lines. She gave marvelous personal service.

When I was in my earliest teens, Ms. Shreenan used to walk by my dad's shop at the end of her day, and I might be pumping gasoline at the curbside in front. "How are you today, young Put?" she would ask with a sweet smile. Celia was very pretty and my recollection is that some of my older male associates were very well aware of that. The telephone company has never given such personal service in all the years since!

Dad was the local dealer for Harley-Davidson motorcycles, and raced them at the Readville Race Track, which was only a few miles away. The movie "Glory" revived its history as the site of the first training camp for black troops in the Civil War.

The war in the 1920s was between Harley-Davidsons – not yet a household word – and Indians, manufactured in our own state of Massachusetts at Springfield.

"If you want to go to the races with us, you will have to dress up," I remember my mother insisting. "If your father wins, they may want you in the picture. I want you to look your best."

She even bought me a new suit for one important race – the first three-piece suit I had ever had. And I tore the pants on the first race day that I wore it.

"Junior," I can remember her exclaiming with disgust.

"How could you do that?" We were approaching the 1929 depression, and damage to new goods was a serious disaster.

Continually during the racing season, Dad had to battle against the perpetual enemy – Indian motorcycles. Races through sand fields on Cape Cod. Races in a hill climb at a towering park slope in Worcester. And the more exciting flat races where the competitors would roar by – lap after lap – in dangerous proximity.

Harley-Davidsons came from Milwaukee – and they still do. As their professional rider, it was his duty to prove that Harleys were superior. He usually managed to do that. He would be overjoyed to note that they still are today.

At the store on Fairmount Avenue, he was in partnership with Henry Sukette – Putnam and Sukette. In addition to selling and servicing motorcycles, they became the first radio dealers in Hyde Park in 1924, and about 1929, the first Pontiac dealers in Greater Boston.

Henry's last name always caused me trouble. We called it Sue-kett with the accent on the last syllable. But the older kids teased me by calling it Suck-it, with the accent on the first syllable. Years went by before I discovered what was so funny about it.

Dad's radio expertise came in handy in March of 1929, when Herbert Hoover was inaugurated President. Dad was able to produce a super heterodyne speaker for the auditorium at the William Barton Rogers Junior High School, so the entire student body could hear the speech as it was delivered.

This was only about eight years after the crystal set, upon which you were lucky to get the first of the powerful stations – KDKA in Pittsburgh. Those produced only little whispers that you could barely hear with your ear cocked to the set. The super heterodyne was an awesome improvement!

Schools were one of the nice features of our neighborhood. I was able to walk just a few blocks to my primary school, elementary school and junior high school – all fabulously located in the years before the automobiles and the super markets led us into urban sprawl. And I could walk to my church, only three blocks away.

The library too was within easy walking distance. I remember sitting on the floor of the second floor room at the Hyde Park Public Library around 1924 while the librarian, Ellen Peterson, read stories to us. I have loved books and stories ever since. My thanks to Ms. Peterson, who was still alive a few years ago – she must have been very young when she enthralled us.

I still remember my teachers' names – Miss Scott, Miss Eager, Miss Waldron, Miss McDowell, Miss Swanson, Miss Hurley, Miss Barry, Miss Farnsworth, etc. They cultivated a close relationship with our parents – some of them had even had our parents in their class a generation earlier.

When they began to give us marks every month or so, I earned mostly As and a few Bs. Miss McDowell, my fourth grade teacher, wrote to my mother:

"Harold is doing very well… He is a joy to have in my class." My mother saved the note, and I still have it!

I was equally joyous about Miss McDowell. She presided over a class of about twenty-five kids in a portable wooden building erected on the grounds of the Elihu Greenwood School. Nowhere near as fancy as most kids have today. Drafty in the winter. Heated only by a pot-bellied stove that had to be stoked with smelly soft coal every few hours. A burly janitor came by frequently to perform that necessary chore.

"Harold. We are going to do Robin Hood, and I want you to be Robin Hood," explained my teacher. "Florence will be Lady Marion."

I could not believe my good fortune. Robin Hood was my favorite story, and Florence Dann was my favorite girl. She was a beautiful blond girl of Dutch ancestry. At the age of ten, girls are a year or two more mature than boys about the relationship between the sexes. I have learned that in recent years as a mentor to 10 and 11-year-olds in Florida. But I note with pleasure that even at the age of ten I was mature enough to appreciate Florence.

I did not realize at the time that all the these ladies were Misses. The state law forbade school committees from hiring married women as public school teachers. Twenty-five years later, when I became a member of the Education Committee of the State Legislature, I had an opportunity to initiate a change. Married women are now needed and welcomed.

Chapter 3

MEET MY MOTHER

The married woman to whom I owe everything was Martha Hyde (Sargent) Putnam, born in 1893 and died in 1931 – when I was just fifteen.

My grandfather, Gilbert Lincoln Sargent (1861-1933), lived next door, and was in touch with us every day of his life. For forty-five years, he was a conductor for the Boston and Albany Railroad – in his senior years in charge of the trip from Boston to Springfield in the evening and back to Boston in the early morning.

Having sired four daughters and no boy, I think he took a special interest in me. We used to sit on his porch at 25 Elm Street often, and I can remember him saying playfully:

"I'm going to bite your ear." I guess he considered that a loving touch, but I never particularly cared for it.

He was very considerate and fatherly, which was helpful because my dad was usually away long hours at the store. Only once did "grampa" get angry at me.

I must have been about seven or eight, and I must have wanted to play monkey. My mother went along with the plan, and prepared a special luncheon for me to carry up a tree. I climbed my grandfather's favorite apple tree, and began peacefully to muNch my delicious lunch.

"Get outta that tree!" Grampa came storming out of the house. I had never seen him angry before, and I was shocked that it was directed at me. Innocent me. Just having a pleasant lunch up in the tree.

Apparently, he had nurtured that tree with loving care. And now that it had matured enough to climb and to have apples, he was more protective of the tree than he was of my boyish feelings. When I fell from another apple tree, this time in Acworth, New Hampshire, I learned that apple trees have very brittle limbs. Grampa was frightened that I had broken an arm or a leg far from home, but thankful that I had learned my lesson at last.

When word came that my mother had died in a hospital in 1931, I remember grampa leaning back in his Morris chair by the bay window and sobbing: "Why couldn't it have been me?" I was awed by the depth of his love for his favorite daughter.

He was to die himself only two years later. The doctor called it asthma. He had trouble breathing, and had to call me to administer something via a hypodermic needle. My diagnosis now is that he died from damaged lungs – damaged by years of picking up tickets in smoking cars blue with the output of cigars and cigarettes. And he never smoked himself.

Grampa's Hupmobile was the first car on Elm Street. And his Timken Silent Automatic Oil Burner was the first of its kind there also. And even though the first agonies of the depression were beginning to be felt by many families, grampa could afford it. And he believed in paying cash. Installment payments – just coming into vogue – never trapped him into buying something he could not afford.

He took us on two memorable trips in his Hupmobile, my father driving. One to visit farm friends in Acworth and one to visit a friend of mother's in Kingston, Ontario – the latter involving my first view of Niagara Falls, which was even more spectacular in the old days than it is now.

Traveling any distance was very different in those days. You were lucky to go a few hundred miles without having to change a tire. There were no places to stop for a leak – you went in the privacy of a row of corn. Occasionally, there were tourist cabins in which you could stop for the night – only one dollar per person as a I recall.

The Burma Shave signs broke the long road monotony with clever rhymes, and grampa could always spot signs to tease a hungry boy:

"Chicken dinners... Chicken dinners one dollar... Hungry? Stop here for a chicken dinner." I don't remember us stopping for many such dinners. The price of gasoline must have been enough of a burden for us – although it was down around nineteen cents in those days.

Grampa lived long enough to see me graduate from Boston Latin School and be accepted by Dartmouth College. He was not a very talkative fellow, but I am confident he was bursting with pride.

He left me one thousand dollars in his will, which was enough to see me through the first year of college. Then I was off and running. He made it possible.

My mother was a very special person. She devoted her life to me. When I was beginning to be old myself, I still met very elderly ladies in Hyde Park who would introduce themselves to me and say:

"You were some baby... Your mother used to wheel you around the block every afternoon... She would be beaming – she was so proud of you."

Her out-of-the-house activities were devoted to the Hyde Park Congregational Church and the Hyde Park Current Events Club.

The church denomination dated back to colonial days, when the first settlers gave themselves the power to create their own congregations and to hire their own clergymen. Her family - the Sargents – were among the first English settlers to navigate the mouth of the Merrimac River and to settle the area around Newbury.

The Current Events Club was the local woman's club, and as a boy I never understood the significance of the name. But I do now! Those ladies were the first feminists. They had fought successfully for the right to vote – a cause they finally won in 1920. And then they were determined to be well-informed about current events, so they organized a woman's club for that purpose. Then and now many women were and are better informed than the men.

Mother was involved in plays and bazaars and lectures and local good works, and usually I went along with her. This was her social life, and for a time it was mine too.

"Want to dress up as George Washington?" she asked one day. Probably it was the choicest part in their play, but it seemed a little sissified to me. I was to dress up in velvet clothes, with an embroidered collar and a three-cornered hat. And I was to be plastered with make-up, at which these ladies were very expert. And they paid good money to rent professional costumes from Boston. I still have a pretty picture of that outfit. I must have been around nine years old.

Another time, she asked: "Think you can learn to do a buck-and-wing? Like Bo Jangles." I am not sure it was Bo Jangles at the time, but it was some famous black tap dancer, and he was very good and very famous. It took considerable practice for me to learn the steps, but it was fun – until the night of the performance and I had to be made up in black face.

The Current Events Club was so successful that it built its own clubhouse, near the center of town – a monument to the power of women in the early days of their political life.

Chapter 4

MY FIRST NAKED LADY

Mother's best buddy at the Hyde Park Current Events Club and in our own neighborhood was a lady named "Kitty." Kitty lived in the first-floor apartment at 65 Arlington Street, where I was born – before we moved two houses away to 27 Elm Street.

Having no children of her own, Kitty was kind of a second mother to me. Both my mother and I were fond of Kitty. Although she seemed matronly to me at the time, I realize with some shock now that she was only in her late twenties and early thirties in the early years of my boyhood.

And she was pretty, voluptuous and vivacious. I came to those conclusions when manhood began to overtake me.

One summer, about 1925, Kitty and her husband shared a cottage with my family in the Cape Cod village of Brewster for two weeks. Brewster is on the bay side of the Cape, where the water is shallow and swimming is possible only at high tides. The sand stretches out for miles, and since Indian days men there have fished with weirs. Fish were caught in the weirs at high tide, and the fishermen emptied them of fish at low tide. Two-wheel horse-drawn wagons were towed out to the weirs to pick up the haul.

But at high tide, it was swim time. We were usually off to the beach. One day, as my mother started off for a swim – anxious to catch a favorable tide – she noticed that Kitty was missing.

"Go back, and tell Kitty we will meet her at the beach," she directed.

I ran back, clambered up the wooden steps of the cottage, let the screen door bang as I entered, and then walked into the bedroom area of the cottage calling "Kitty."

No response! Her bedroom door was open, and I looked in! Kitty was standing, totally nude, just stepping into her one-piece bathing suit. She was partially facing me – leaning slightly forward – a pose I learned later was the favorite modeling position for naked ladies in the paintings of Maxfield Parrish.

She made no effort to cover up, and she showed no sign of dressing in haste. Surely, she had heard my noisy entrance. She smiled, then said softly, "Tell Mother I'll be right along."

That was the first time I ever saw a female totally nude. Probably Kitty is long gone now, but as I have become more knowledgeable about such matters, I like to think that she deliberately contributed to my education. I thank her for it!

Now that I am better informed about other cultures, and have studied assiduously how they inform their children about the joys of sex, I am not convinced that our befuddled non-system is the best way. Why learn from equally ignorant kids, when someone like Kitty is around to impart basic knowledge in a loving way?

Those were the days! Happy days – and no adult problems. Wollaston Beach was only a few miles away from Hyde Park, and in summer weather we headed there often. After swimming, in what was then clean water and is now often polluted, we stopped for ice cream – homemade by the original Howard Johnson in the basement of his drugstore. He not only dished out the best ice cream ever made to that date, but he gave you a generous scoop – a rounded scoop for a nickel but a giant volcano-shaped scoop for a dime.

At our corner store in those days, we could get a scoop for five cents, a double-decker for a dime or a totally gorgeous sundae for fifteen cents. And the fudge sauce and whipped cream NEVER came out of a can!

In the late 1920s, my mother sent me off to spend the summers with a retired doctor and his wife on a Maine farm. I was only eleven and twelve years ago. And then for many summers from 1928 to 1932, I reveled in the Indian life of Camp Waldron on Lake Winnisquam in Meredith, New Hampshire.

In the summer of 1933, I began four years of college preparatory study at Boston Latin School, the oldest public school in America, and one with the most demanding academic requirements. I can remember crying over my homework – just once!

The boy was on the way to becoming a man!

Chapter 5

DOWN ON THE FARM

"Do you want to spend the summer on Doctor Carter's farm?" my mother asked, after reading the letter from Maine.

"Sure. Can I?"

"You won't get homesick?"

"No. I don't think so."

My mother and I were devoted to each other. Decisions like this were made by her – my father was always busy at the store, often from 9 a.m. to 9 at night. She showed no hesitancy in sending me away for the entire summer – and I was only about ten or eleven years old at the time.

The current crop of mothers seems to me more concerned with their own companionship than they are with developing self-reliance and independence in their children. Perhaps a harsh judgment, but in my case, I am sure that my mother thought it was time I became acquainted with a man's work, and that it was not too early for me to start.

Also, the professional stature of my host had something to do with it. Dr. Curtis Carter was a graduate of Harvard Medical School. He was in his 60s in the middle of the 1920s, and had abandoned the practice of medicine – my conclusion now is that he was a victim of burnout. He no longer wanted to tolerate the stresses of a medical practice.

He had selected a small farm about ten miles west of Belfast, Maine, and about three miles north of Route 3 which connects Belfast with the state capital at Augusta. Even Route 3 was still a dirt road in those days, and the road into the farm is still a dirt road today.

The farm was located in Morrill, about a mile from Center Montville, where there was then a store and today there is almost nothing. The whole area has fallen on more desolate times. On the level farming plane between the north ridge and Ruffingham Meadows, the dance hall, and the Howe, Ring and Hall farmhouses are all gone. The Mehurens I knew are in the local cemetery.

Only the Carter farm stands improved from the old days. An ambitious and hardworking young man has restored the Cape Cod farmhouse, built a fine new barn and erected a stand of tall fir trees that shelter the buildings from the ferocity of the winter winds. A toast to him!

A toast also to the MBNA Corporation, which is pumping new life into the old port city of Belfast. Its heyday was in the time of the great sailing ships. Some of the enriched masters of those ships built spectacular homes on the upland back from the waterfront. The houses are still there, but the riches have gone.

I first visited the thriving waterfront of Belfast in 1924, when I was only eight. My aunt Viola and her new husband, Warren, took me on an overnight run from Boston on the steamer BELFAST. Thrilling adventure for a small boy. Those coastal steamers suffered an occasional disaster, which made future voyages uneconomic – up to this time. But now that navigational instruments are awesome in their efficiency and their accuracy, there is no good reason why such spectacular and restful voyages could not be resumed.

The great liners that compete for Caribbean tourists are running out of suitable destinations. I favor a resumption of service to the New England coast – Newport, Boston, Salem, Newburyport, Portsmouth, Portland, Rockland, Belfast and Bar Harbor are ideal destinations – not only spectacular in their scenery but rich in colonial history.

Dr. Carter's wife, Sally, turned out to be the mother of my new uncle, Warren. Dr. Carter was Sally's second husband. I did not get that figured out until I was well along in being a grown man.

Doc was a super farmer and a congenial friend. He was overjoyed to have me as an able-bodied helper. Sally I remember as a bit on the grumpy side. But she was a great cook, and there was always something good brewing on the cast-iron kitchen stove, fueled around the clock by wood that we cut and chopped up into suitable pieces by hand. In fact, my left hand still shows a V at the base of my index finger, the victim of a sharp ax and an errant blow.

Our labors and our risks were duly rewarded by Sally. I still place her strawberry shortcake at the top of my list of great desserts. Her homemade shortcake was baked in a 12-inch circular pan, and then sliced horizontally through the middle, creating a first layer and a top layer to be drowned in the sweetest strawberries I ever ate. Made sweeter by the fact that I picked them in our own field. And Sally topped the whole thing with shipped cream, straight from their Jersey cow and the separator in the back room!

For some of that shortcake about once a week, I could forgive Sally for an occasional grumpy spell.

To reach the Carter farm in those days from Boston was not all that easy. A three-hour run today took about seven as I remember it in the old days. Route 1 most of the way, right through the center of each village and farm. But I do not remember having to stop overnight on the way, and I do not remember any flat tires – a tribute to my father's expertise with motor vehicles.

At the high point of land east of Augusta and near the end of our journey, he would say:

"Watch out now. On the left you may be able to see the farm."

It was pitch black at the end of our journey. How could we see the farm?

Dad had arranged with Sally to place a lantern in the kitchen window, which he hoped would be visible from the height of the roadway overlooking the Ruffingham Meadows. I have made this trip with my uncle in his open "flivver" – an early four-door Ford. But I think on this trip we were riding in my grandfather's Hupmobile, the predecessor to the Oldsmobiles and Pontiacs we used just before the disaster of the depression.

"Watch on the left. Way off in the distance."

"There it is," I exulted. A tiny yellow light in the midst of the darkness of the isolated farm land. It must have been a good three miles away, and probably a good half hour from our arrival. Dad blinked our car lights – the prearranged signal to Sally and Doc that we were almost there.

Near a little country store about ten miles east of Belfast, we had to leave Route 3 and strike north onto dirt roads – and the first stretch was up a steep hill and it was always gouged out by the latest rain. All of this was wonderland for a city boy – a cooper's farm on the left, where the farmer spent most of his time making barrels, a brook at the low point on the dirt road that was good for trout fishing, and then Mr. Howe's farm. His place was always the neatest and most productive in the area.

Just before you turned onto the dirt road to the Carter farm, there was a dance hall. It was never jumping with activity when I was there, but I heard stories that it was a lively community center in the fall and spring months. I doubt that they could have kept warm there in the savage winters that swept across that farming plain.

The Carter farmhouse was a typical Cape Cod structure, with a woodshed attached in the back and a separate barn where Doc kept a huge horse named Charlie. Fields stretched a quarter of a mile in all directions – most of them mowed and a few cultivated with potatoes and other vegetables.

The nearest farm – the Mehuren's – was a half-mile away on the dirt road. Sally fled in that direction at the first sign of a thunderstorm, dragging me along with her.

"Let's go. Quick," she insisted, quivering with fear. Doc – much less fearful – would dutifully trudge along after us.

My attention had never been called to thunder and lightning before that. But they were more audible and more visible in the open country of a Maine farm. Lightning stabbed farms and churches with surprising frequency – so there was real reason for Sally's concern.

The first storm after my arrival convinced me that they do have some real humdingers in those parts in the summertime – and they were scary at night, when the flashes converted the inky darkness into daylight. As the lightning crackled overhead and the shards stabbed down into the darkness, it did seem to be kind of a warning that someone was out to get YOU.

I no longer blamed Sally for thinking so!

Chapter 6

SEX ON THE FARMS

Doc and I were more concerned about running the farm than we were about lightning. We were hardworking companions from dawn to dusk.

"Ever ride a horse?" he asked that first summer.

"Nope."

"Ever run a hay rake?"

"Nope."

"Do you think you could ride Charlie-horse, and guide him down the rows while I hold the plow?"

"Sure." Doc boosted me up onto this gigantic horse – the biggest horse that I had ever seen. I picked up the reigns, and steered Charlie into the first row of a large field. He was a bright horse – at last more experienced than I. So he needed little guidance and we pulled the plow into row after row in a large field. I liked this new-found feeling of power surging under me, and the growing proof that teamwork produced more efficient results than folks working alone. At least on a farm, Doc and Charlie and I were a useful team.

I don't ever recall being tired, despite towing the plow while on Charlie-horse, running a hayrake, tramping the load on a hay wagon, then driving it home and unloading it in the barn, hoeing vegetables or cutting and burning brush to enlarge some of the fringe fields. I liked it in this man's world.

Sometimes when we paused to take a leak, Doc would look

down at my tiny penis, and ask, "How's Ikey today?"? I never understood his interest. Ikey always seemed quite normal and uninteresting to me!

But now and then something really interesting would occur – like the birth of a calf.

"Bessie is getting ready to calf," Doc noted. "Better go see how she's doing."

We walked across a field, and down into the pasture, looking carefully upon each side of the cowpath and especially in the woods that shielded the grassy areas.

"There she is," Doc pointed out.

There she was – next to a bloody mass. A newborn calf? It seemed impossible that this mass of blood and guts could come to life – yet little legs with tiny hoofs were beginning to uncoil.

"Can we help her?"

"Not as well as the mother." What the calf could do for itself was astonishing. And what the mother could do to help was touching – literally touching by lapping and figuratively touching by a show of love and concern.

The calf moved its head. The calf stretched its long and ungainly legs. The mother licked her clean. Then the calf stood up – all by itself. I was speechless – awed by this first experience with the birthing process.

I still did not understand how such miracles were achieved, and Doc was not as much help as he could have been. When I saw cows trying to mount the back of another cow – doggie-style – I asked Doc why they did that.

His reply. "Better ask Freddie." Freddie was a state ward, who lived with the Mehurens next door. He was my only summer playmate – but one or two years older than I and a bit of a wiseguy in my book. I was not keen about asking Freddie about anything – and I have always regretted that Doc, the Harvard Medical School authority, did not choose to answer my good and timely question.

Things have not changed very much in the field of sex education in the last seventy years. Adults are still satisfied to have their kids pick up their knowledge of sex from fresh kids.

When I did get a chance to ask Freddie, his reply was, "They're trying to fuck. But tough luck... They are both females." That left me as much in the dark as ever.

Doc shared my curiosity about things sexual, but he was not very forthcoming with explanations. One day we visited the Howes down the road, and were escorted out to the barn to see a new pony that they had acquired for their granddaughter, Jeannette. I was expressing my boyhood glee, when I looked down and noticed that something awesome was happening to his cock! It was extending to the length and thickness of a baseball bat!

Doc had noticed it too. He leaned over and whispered to me: "I wonder if Jeannette has seen that?" I was too young to get the connection. What did the pony's prick have to do with Jeannette? Took me years to figure that out.

I was not particularly fond of Freddie, but he did contribute some useful knowledge to my summer experience. We swam in the brook and swung on a rope over the water. He could show me trout, waggling around in the cold water – and he took me to favorite fishing haunts of Ben Ames Williams, then a nationally-famous writer for the Saturday Evening Post.

And he introduced me to Millie, a shy, half-starved creature who lived next door and suffered under a ruthless father – who beat his horses and did not seem any kinder to his child. That first summer at the Carter farm Millie's only clothing was a flour bag – with holes cut in it for the neck and arms. She was a forlorn specimen.

But the next summer, something had caused a transformation in Millie. She was a little heavier, and not so starved-looking. And the flour bag was gone in favor of a simple sheath dress. She seemed a little rounder and a lot healthier. And Freddie seemed more interested in her than ever.

"Let's go down to Millie's pasture," Freddie invited me one

warm summer afternoon. "I'll show you something interesting."

We climbed a rough, old fence and started across the pasture – heading for a pine grove at the far end and stepping carefully to avoid both the new and the old cowflaps. Then I noticed Millie – far down the pasture, but heading for the same destination.

"Hi," she said softly, when we met in the grove.

"You look nice," I think I contributed, feeling a little guilty for my critical conclusions of a year ago.

But Freddie seemed to be in charge, and each of them seemed to know why they had come there. Millie slipped out of her dress, carefully placed it on the pine needles and laid down upon it.

I had seen a naked lady once before, but this was my first exposure to a naked girl! In my virgin innocence, I had no idea why Freddie had planned this and no idea what came next! I watched in awe.

Freddie quickly shucked off his pants. "Now watch this," he instructed me. "This is what the cows were up to. But this is the real thing."

I couldn't miss the fact that he "had a bone on." Probably me too. Erections must have happened to me before this scene, but in total privacy. I had never seen one upon another human being. Freddie fondled it lovingly. It seemed long and thin and white. I have wondered since if this startling demonstration by Freddie occurred in his pre-pubertal or post-pubertal years.

He covered Millie quickly, and she submitted quietly– her big eyes looking up at me as Freddie set about his task. I discovered that teenage girls grow bigger eyes and longer eyelashes, and their bodies get rounder. They are no longer as strange and uninteresting as they were in earlier years.

I compliment myself that her eyes were saying to me: "I wish it were you."

I don't remember the act being all that pleasurable for them. I don't remember if full penetration was achieved, or if either party came. But when Freddie lifted off her, he did say: "Wanna try her?"

"No thanks." I don't know yet why I declined. A man should not pass up such opportunities, but I guess I was not yet a man. It was all too new and strange to me, and I guess I concluded that my mother would not approve.

Almost seventy years later that little valley of subsistence farms is still full of warm memories for me: the towering elm trees not yet crippled with Dutch elm disease, the brook not yet polluted with industrial or human waste, the pure cool water of a deep well, the friendships among families totally dependent upon each other, the telephone lines upon which you could listen to your neighbor's business, the going to the kitchen window to check out any car that occasionally passed by. And the cute Jersey calf that one year later was an awkward big old cow.

My mother had several good reasons for sending me up there for two summers, but not the least was the fact that Doc Carter was a highly-trained physician. I think that Mama would have like to have me go that route, but college chemistry taught me that the physical sciences were not the route for me!

Doc recovered from his burnout. In those days I think they called it a nervous breakdown. He always seemed perfectly normal to me, and the citizens of Montague, Massachusetts, came to the same conclusion in the 1930s and begged him successfully to come back to practice and to be their town doctor.

For a boy going through those turbulent years of 10 to 12 that Maine farm experience was of great value to me. I learned to enjoy hard, physical labor. I appreciated the experiences that my ancestors had suffered in clearing the Colonial lands and eking out an existence from a harsh environment.

I absorbed the old Yankee virtues of independence and self-reliance.

And I learned that a teenage girl is very different – and very special!

Chapter 7

SUMMER CAMP

By the summer of 1928 my mother had agreed to send me to a boys' camp for the first time. Through my Hyde Park Congregational Church we booked the first two weeks in August at Camp Waldron on Lake Winnisquam in Meredith, New Hampshire.

The camp was located on some 500 acres of virgin forest at the base of Mount Ladd, and southern-exposed to the lake and Mounts Gunstock and Belknap on the distant horizon. It had been purchased by the City Missionary Society of Boston sometime after World War I, and had been chopped out of the wilderness with considerable efforts by Congregational ministers and their devoted lay supporters.

The Society dated back to pre-Civil War years, and had been created to help the children of Boston. It was housed at 14 Beacon Street in Boston, the Congregational House that also contained the American Board of Commissioners for Foreign Missions - from whence had been sent many of the original missionaries dispatched to China and India and to the Hawaiian Islands.

My church participated in this momentous decision by agreeing to put up the money for my two weeks' tuition - $25. per week as I recall - less than one-tenth of the cost of such joyful vacations today. I had earned this support by faithfully serving throughout the church year as a "messenger boy," delivering the weekly church news letter to some thirty homes in my neighborhood.

"Are you sure you want to go?", my mother asked.

"Sure."

"You get a nice ride on a train. But you can't get homesick after you get there."

No danger. I did not get homesick on two summers on the Carter Farm in Maine, so I did not see any chance of my getting homesick in the exciting place and program that awaited me in the summer of 1928. Train ride! Wonderful!

I had experienced only one train ride to that point in my life, and that one had almost literally knocked my socks off. My grandpa Sargent had taken me with him on one of his night runs from Boston to Springfield.

Before our departure from the South Station in Boston, he had taken me forward from his conductor post to inspect the monster engine that huffed and steamed several cars down the platform. It seemed as long as a football field and as charged as a rocket ready for launching. I could feel the throb of pent-up power as my grandfather lifted me up to the cab.

He introduced me to the engineer and the fireman, and I still remember their names - Bennett and Marshall ! But I have never forgiven them either. In explaining their functions and the operation of this devilish contraption, the fireman stepped on the lever that opened the firebox - and I almost fell with horror into a raging inferno. I never forgave them for the scare!

But trains still held a fascination for me, and they were only beginning to fall out of common usage as motor vehicles became more powerful and more reliable. The ride to camp took me from the North Station up to the cities along the Merrimac River, and then up the Merrimac Valley to Franklin, and then up the Winnipesaukee River Valley to Lake Winnisquam and Laconia. Not until decades later did I learn that this was the up-river route that many of our ancestors had taken to settle the interior of New Hampshire. The first scouts from the Massachusetts Bay Colony to Lake Winnisquam and Lake Winnipesaukee had taken the same route - by much slower means of transportation.

Our merry band of Greater Boston Congregational boys were herded onto "The Alouette," - so named because it must have continued on to Montreal. But it took us to the station in downtown Laconia - then and now a beautiful, livable city. I don't think we realized until that point that Camp Waldron was unreachable by motor vehicle. You could drive to Meredith, and then take a dirt road west for about five miles - but you would still be a half-mile from the lakeside camp.

Camp in the summer was reachable only by boat. All of its construction materials and food supplies came in only over the ice in winter or by boat in the summer. The boat was an open launch, capable of carrying about thirty boys, and it awaited us at the end of Oak Street on the shore of Winnisquam.

The landing was only about a quarter of a mile from the railroad station, and I think we must have walked it through the neat streets of downtown Laconia and out through a tree-lined residential area. The boat and two war canoes awaited us - the canoes to carry our baggage.

Fully loaded at last with boisterous boys, the boat snaked its way north (towing the war canoes!) over the six miles of open water to the dock at the camp. For a boy who grew up in a fully-developed section of a big city, all that I saw now resembled my heart's desire - an Indian village. A beach, canoes, trails through the dense woods, a look-out of granite high above the lake - and occasionally the lonely cry of a loon.

The counsellors nourished our fantasy. We were members of the "Abenaki Nation." We were divided into two tribes of boys under 14 - Naumkeags and Penagogs. The boys over 14 were inducted into the Penacooks or the Aquadoctins. Not until years later did I learn that there really was an "Abenaki Nation," and it stretched across what is now northern New England from the eastern shore of Lake Champlain into what is now Maine.

And there really were tribes whose names we carried. In

fact, "Naumkeag" was the Indian name for the area along the Massachusetts coast that my English ancestors called "Salem."

Those of us who were assigned to the Naumkeag tribe were dispatched to the campfire circle for a secret pow-wow. No councillors. Only twenty-five 12-year-old boys, few of whom knew the boys sitting next to them. Our order - choose a Sachem!

I came out of that meeting "Sachem of the Naumkeags." I still do not know how or why it happened. It was the first time that my peers had ever bestowed upon me the mantle of leadership. I found that I liked it!

Our tribe raced in a war canoe. We fielded a baseball team. And we put forth our best efforts in a track meet on "Field Day."

We excelled in everything except swimming, and there I could not be much help to them. The basic requirement that we swim fifty yards was a formidable challenge to me, and without completing it we were barred from the use of boats and canoes.

"Come on. You can do it. Dog-paddle is OK - just keep working away at it," counselled the swimming instructor. But a muscular 12-year-old boy is only slightly more buoyant than a rock, and it required some furious dog-paddling to keep me afloat during a 50-yard swim. Eventually I satisfied the Senior Lifesaver requirements of the American Red Cross, but it was the most difficult and least pleasurable achievement of my athletic career.

In baseball I was more at home. And it was the favorite game of the Reverend Sidney Lovett, the pastor of the Mount Vernon Congregational Church at Beacon Street and Massachusetts Avenue in Boston, and "Uncle Sid" was the respected "god-father" of the camp. I think he was the most ardent supporter of the camp from its earliest days - beginning right after World War I.

We played pick-up games every time he visited camp, and we came to know each other well and to enjoy our baseball competition over several summers. Our show-down came in a later summer when I had reached 15, and Uncle Sid had been promoted to Chaplain of Yale University in New Haven. He offered to bring his Yale team with him, and challenged our best camp players.

"We have a great pitcher," Sid admitted to us. "He has been pitching for Yale." He did not tell us until later that Ted Horton had also been signed by the New York Yankees!

My camp team looked like the hitless wonders. We had never played against a pitcher with such speed and control and "stuff." The score of Sid's team mounted, and ours remained at zero - until my last bat!

Summers of canoeing had produced some special strength in my shoulders and arms - good for power at the plate in a game of baseball. And finally, in my fourth at bat, I was no longer awed by the speed of Ted Horton. I was determined to stand in the batter's box, and give his offerings my best swing.

I caught one of his faster pitches on the "sweet" part of my bat, and the ball went soaring out to the Ellison Cabin "perch" for a home run! Years later - when I knew that home runs in the major leagues usually exceed 385 yards, I went back to measure this historic drive. I guessed it to be around 400 yards. But nature had recovered the baseball field, and I could no longer find it!

We lost that game something like 18 to 1. When I next saw the Rev. Sidney Lovett we were both at the graduation ceremony of Dartmouth College in 1937 - I to get my A.B. degree and Sid to receive an Honorary Degree. I don't remember the carefully chosen words on his encomium, but they should have included special mention of his prowess as a role model for ambitious young boys.

Several other counsellors contributed to these warm memories of my youth. Dr. Harold Henry Hamilton, while a student at Harvard Medical School, kept us healthy and charmed us with his guitar music and his lively singing. He spent his professional life as the beloved town doctor in Plymouth, Massachusetts.

The Rev. Edwin Tupper Anthony I had known first when

he was a boy at Boston Latin School, about three years ahead of me. He had been one of the winners at "declamation" competitions. I found him at camp when he was training for the ministry, and then he filled the important job of bursar. He bought the food for our hungry horde, and kept the books.

The Rev. Edgar Bruce Wilson was the boys' worker at the City Missionary Society. He kept us enchanted with camp-related activities during the winter. Later he was the Methodist minister at churches in Concord and Lebanon, New Hampshire.

Charles E. Gary was the cook in my camp days, and has been a life-long friend. The City Missionary Society had located Charlie during his student days at Hampton Institute in Virginia - requesting a young cook who would be good in athletics and inspirational to boys. Hampton had been founded after the Civil War years to educate young black boys, and much of the money for the venture had come from Boston Congregational abolitionists. Charlie was a great product of that school - and also a super baseball player.

He convinced us that black boys could be great baseball players - about twenty years ahead of Jackie Robinson. Charlie was the only one of us who ever hit a baseball that wound up in the lake. It had to roll about the last twenty yards - but it was still a world-record slam.

And I do not recall any racial prejudice. Charlie was the only black in camp in those days. He visited my home in Boston one year, en route back to Virginia, and I do not remember any problems.

"Pete" Knight (Charles Lewis Knight, Jr. of West Roxbury and Dartmouth '32) was my special friend and mentor in canoeing.

Rev. Ed Wilson had told us one winter that he was going to produce a "real live Indian" on the waterfront next summer.

"Yes, sir. A real Indian."

We were awed with the possibility. We expected a weathered, dark-skinned brave, with jet black hair and dressed in fringed deer skin.

"Where's the Indian?", we were quick to ask "Uncle Ed" when we arrived at camp the next summer. He presented Pete Knight - muscular and tanned, OK; but Yankee, Protestant and blond! We really never forgave Uncle Ed for that "story," even though Pete proved to possess all the qualities we wanted in a real Indian.

Uncle Ed's excuse was: "Well, he really IS an Indian. He is in the Dartmouth class of 1932, and they call Dartmouth students Indians."

Pete had his own racing canoe, and we paddled it back to Boston in the summer of 1932 - about 200 miles in five days - a trip that no-one has tackled since. And in the summer of 1933, we paddled a double kayak around New England - nearly 2000 miles in 66 days - another trip that no-one has tackled since.

But in those earliest years at camp, much of the speculation was about the Loyalty Medal. "Who do you think will get the Loyalty Medal?" It was awarded to one boy in the under-14 camp in each camp term, and it was presented by the Camp Director at the "Farewell Feed" that marked the last night in camp.

In my second summer - 1929 - we assembled in The Lodge for the final night. Outside the porch windows the lake glimmered in the setting sun. About 100 boys piled in, scrunching the rough benches on the wooden floor. And great food being served family style on the crowded tables. But who would get the Loyalty Medal?

The Camp Director, Rev. Everett Moore Baker, presided at the head table. He was a handsome 1925 graduate of Dartmouth - distinguished, experienced and a moving speaker - although it seems now as though he could only have been about twelve years older than I.

The dinner served. A few speeches concluded. Some athletic awards made. Uncle Ev rose to speak. The Loyalty Medal !

"The camp is now proud to award its highest honor to one of our campers. Each year we award it to the boy who seems to us to have been outstanding in all the activities of the camp - and who embodies our highest ideals. . . Will Harold Putnam please come forward."

I still remember where I sat in that stark common room on that evening. I still remember walking to the head table. I still remember Uncle Ev giving me an affectionate and fatherly greeting. And I still have the Loyalty Medal. It carries the head of an Indian brave - and above it the word "Loyalty" and below it the words "Camp Waldron of the Abenaki Nation."

On the back is engraved: - "1929 and 1930"...

Rev. Edward Moore Baker became the Dean of Students at the Massachusetts Institute of Technology, and a leader in the international students movement. He suffered an untimely death in a plane crash while returning from an international conference.

I grew from boy to youth to man at Camp Waldron. I loved the woods and the lake and the mountains, the Indian lore, the inspirational activities and the exceptional leadership. I went from camper to junior counsellor to senior counsellor.

And both at camp and in high school, I lived in an all-boy world. But around the age of 16, I began to appreciate girls.

I had met Barbara Wales at the City Missionary Society when I went in each year to sign my counsellor contract. I was well aware that she was pretty, charming and intelligent. Perhaps three or four years older than I.

When she visited one summer – it must have been when I was 16 – I summoned up enough nerve to invite her to go to the movies with me. The movies were about ten miles away in Laconia, and the only way to get there and back was by canoe. And it would take from about 5 p.m. until midnight. Would she like to go?

"Sure. That would be nice."

I made her a comfortable seat in the bottom of the canoe,

and then paddled almost silently to the dock in Laconia. We enjoyed the movie, and devoured a hot fudge sundae – where did I get the money? And then paddled home, the canoe quietly cutting the velvet darkness and only the cry of the loon to be heard in the stillness of the summer night.

As the canoe reached the beach, Barbara spoke up: "Let's take a skinny dip!"

I wasn't prepared for such a mature suggestion. I had never been skinny- dipping at night with a man or boys – let alone a lovely woman. I had never seen a full-grown girl naked. Even though it was around midnight and the camp was asleep, suppose someone came down to the beach – while we were in the water. Suppose someone heard about it, and I was fired for such a daring act?

I don't recall answering "Yes" or "No." It was my duty to get the paddles and the canoe back on their racks, and I was strong enough then to hoist the canoe onto my shoulders and carry it to its place under the lodge.

By the time I returned to the beach, Barbara had shucked her clothes and was swimming out to the raft about forty yards offshore. I observed that she was a fine swimmer, and that was about all I could observe. My life-saver training convinced me that no-one should swim alone – especially at night, so I doffed my clothes and plunged into the lake after her.

As I approached the raft and came up for one final breath of air, I had a brief glimpse of my naked Valkyrie etched in the moonlight. When I reached the raft, she had slipped back into the water and was on the way to the beach.

She was back into her dress by the time I returned to the beach, and sedately I walked her back to her cabin. I never even took her by the hand. I never even kissed her good-night.

Those were great summers on the shore of Lake Winnisquam. I can still hear the strains of "Taps" coming from Bill Lockwood's bugle, and sifting through the rustling trees:

Day is done,
Gone the sun,
From the lakes,
From the woods, and
From the sky,
All is well,
Safely rest,
God is nigh.

A good-night kiss to Barbara, wherever she is, and a bless-ing to those "Uncles" – Ev, Ham, Pete, Charlie, Ed and Sid – who enriched the days of my youth.

Chapter 8

BOSTON LATIN SCHOOL
1929-1933

My mother sent me off to Boston Latin School in 1929 at the age of 13, separating me from my Hyde Park school-mates and for the next eight years from girls.

Latin School was all boys – even all male teachers – in those days, and so was Dartmouth College.

Boston Latin School was the first public school in America, organized in 1635 in a city that was only five years old. Its purpose was to prepare the most promising boys for Harvard College, not yet up and running.

Then and now it was and is one of the toughest college preparatory schools in America. I can remember coming off almost all As in junior high school into competition that pressured me to survive, and even crying over my homework during the first few weeks. Something like 98 per cent of all graduates go on to four-year colleges, and a large percentage continue further through graduate schools.

The school began on School Street in downtown Boston, only a block away from where Benjamin Franklin was born. It was nearly one hundred years old when Ben studied there. Unfortunately, he did not graduate – his family moved to Philadelphia.

In September of 1929, at the age of 13, mother sent me off to my first independent trolley ride, armed with student "car checks" to pay the fare and a brown bag to satisfy my noontime hunger. The school was about nine miles from Hyde Park, and the trolley ride took about one hour each way.

The Hyde Park trolley clattered along Hyde Park avenue into the Forest Hills Station, where we transferred to a trolley that rolled through Jamaica Plain to Huntington Avenue, and then Longwood Avenue. Longwood was my stop.

I had never been in that part of the city before. I had never seen the school to which I was being sent. I had no idea of the world fame of both the school and its neighbors – but I do now.

I felt as though I were in the Valley of the Gods – surrounded by the largest and most imposing buildings I had ever seen. Girls Latin School to the right and the Angell Memorial Hospital to my left, one of the first and finest animal hospitals in the world. Then the Massachusetts College of Pharmacy and the Boston Lying-in Hospital. And then the largest collection of identical buildings I had ever seen – silent and imposing – the Harvard Medical School.

"Keep going to Avenue Louis Pasteur," my mother had instructed me. "Then the school is on your right." And across the street was the arch-rival – Boston English High School.

A stream of boys lined up for the registration desk – I heard lots of Jewish names and Irish names, not very common in the still white, Protestant enclave of Hyde Park.

"Putnam? . . . Mr. Cheetham's room. First floor." I was on my way – with no girls!

Florence must have been sent to Hyde Park High School. I had been devoted to Florence since the fourth grade, when an observant teacher had selected her to be "Lady Marion" to my "Robin Hood."

And Charlotte and Rita must have wound up there also – just when they had changed from caterpillars into butterflies! The scrawny girls had been transformed into curvaceous maidens – in just that last year of junior high school!

When I contemplate those eight years of asceticism now , my conclusion is that I grew up bright, but considerably behind the norm in sexual development. I agonized until I was seventeen – in this world of super education – before anyone told me the fundamental truth that masturbation is common and normal in young boys. Even young girls!

And I remained a virgin until 23. If I could do that over again, and were given a vote, I would choose the easy pre-marital relationships that are common today.

But back to school in 1929, and the strict curriculum of Latin, English, Mathematics, German and French. And I hated languages! I hated German and French and the rote method by which they were taught, and I never was convinced that I would have any use for them. And I never understood why I was forced to translate Cicero and Virgil.

I could figure out that Caesar reported that all Gaul was divided into three parts – but so what? I didn't know where Gaul was, or why Caesar was concerned about it, or what difference it made if it were divided into three parts. And nobody made a case for taking Latin in the first place – every student, every year for close to three hundred years when I labored there.

I would have been inclined more favorably toward the complicated Latin text, if someone had explained to me that it was the official language of the Roman Empire for something like a thousand years. And my boyhood ears would have pricked up if I had been advised that it was the official language of England – my homeland – from around 42 A.D. until Chaucer, some eleven hundred years later, began creating what we now call "English."

P.S. The current Head Master of Boston Latin School, Michael Contompasis, advises me that Latin was used commonly from 80 B.C. until the 15th century!

Roman coins are still found in Putnam fields just east of Aylesbury in Buckinghamshire County, England, and the ancestral village of Puttenham (still pronounced "Putnam") is described in

William the Conqueror's Domesday Book of 1086 in Latin!

I suffered through the language for four years, and finally wound up in "Jeff" Winslow's class on the third floor of the school in my senior year. I recognize now that "Jeff" was probably a direct descendant of one of the first Governors of the Massachusetts Bay Colony, but he and Latin were still painful bores to me.

The most interesting part of his Latin class was the view to the east out the windows – looking down on the recreational backyard of Simmons College, then an all-girls' school. My hormonal changes then – at age 17 – were so compelling that I could not keep my mind on Latin when attractive young ladies were bouncing around in skimpy clothing just outside the window.

I flunked the "Jeff" Winslow Latin class in my senior year, and that almost kept me out of college – until I rescued myself with a high mark in the College Board examination.

I doubt that the curriculum has changed very much in the 360-plus years of Latin School history. In addition to the detested languages, they still insist upon super skills in reading, writing and arithmetic. In senior English, students were flunked for a single error in grammar or spelling. Not many seniors in other schools could pass in these times, if subjected to such a demanding requirement.

Everything at Boston Latin School was serious business. Students who did not take their work seriously were quickly bounced back to schools that could be satisfied with an ordinary education. Even in sports – we were expected to win the city championships, and we usually did.

At football, I could hold my own in Hyde Park with any of the lads my own age, but Coach Tom Fitzgerald at Latin School always seemed to have a few half-backs that were bigger or faster than I was. In those days, we played both ways – offense and defense. Size was important to the line-backing and speed was essential to the running.

But "Fitzy" made sure that I won my letter by putting me

into the Thanksgiving Day game against English High School at Fenway Park in Boston.

"Fenway Park" – this was hallowed ground! I had watched baseball games there in my boyhood years as a member of the "Knot-Hole Gang." The Red Sox club not only admitted us free, but they trotted out their players to instruct us. This was back in the days of Jimmy Foxx and Joe Cronin. And of a center-fielder named Tom Oliver, whose strange batting stance I chose not to adopt. He used to stand in the batter's box almost facing the pitcher – he was lucky to hit as well as he did!

But I never got into a major game until the closing minutes of that city championship game.

"Putnam," I heard Coach Fitzgerald say. "Get in there. Line-backer. Right side." Latin was struggling to hold a slim lead – with about three minutes left to play.

It was awesome to look up at the Fenway Park stands from the playing field. Only the greatest baseball players in the land were privileged to have this view – plus a few high school football players on special days. I knew that the football was in play somewhere near what normally was the pitching mound. I had watched Walter Johnson and Lefty Grove work their Hall of Fame magic in that spot.

But I had no time to reminisce. I knew that this was the crowning moment of my football career. Coach had rarely given me an opportunity to carry the ball, but at least he had some confidence in me as a defender.

I heard the English quarterback call his signals. I watched the backs line up to take the ball. I keyed on Dick Freno – just named City of Boston All-Scholastic half-back!

Freno had the ball – as I expected – and he was heading my way. English had figured – as I expected – that a new kid in the backfield would be a vulnerable target. And I figured I could only live once – at least once on the sacred turf of Fenway Park. And this would probably be the end of my football career.

I ploughed across the line of scrimmage – why wait for him to reach me? Aimed for the spot where Freno would have to cut up field, and hit him waist-high, with my arms around both knees.

Three-yard loss! The peak of my football career!

At hockey, I did much better. The coach put together a team that won the city championship in 1931 and 1932. I played left defense and earned the nickname, "Icicle" – I guess because of my coolness when bigger brutes came storming in my direction.

That was a very special team – not only because we could beat any other school-boys, but because they were successful scholars. In these days when many professional athletes can hardly speak English, how about a hockey team upon which every member except one became a lawyer – Tom Bilodeau, Fred Roche, Leo Glynn, George Mahoney, Freddie Moore, Charlie Carroll and Harold Putnam.

On that first team, only John Ryan, my team-mate on defense, did not become a lawyer. But his sister was Kathleen Ryan Dacey – one of the first prominent women lawyers in Boston! Forty years after my hockey playing with John, I had the privilege of appointing Kathleen to be an Administrative Judge in the Social Security Administration – over the dead body of the Nixon Administration!

"She's a Democrat."

"Yes," I replied, "and she has superior qualifications and she has met all the requirements."

Washington Nixonites went along with the appointment angrily, and then as her first assignment dispatched her to a midwest city more than one thousand miles from her home. Nice fellows – that Nixon crowd!

But Kathleen stuck it out. Eventually worked her way back to Boston, and served with distinction for many years.

Our hockey team played at the Boston Arena, the original home of the Boston Bruins, and now the home rink of Northeastern University. In the interim, the state preserved it as a haven of schoolboy hockey – thanks to one of my most successful legislative moves and the approval of Governor Christian A. Herter around 1954.

High on the list of my Latin School memories sixty-three years after graduation are "declamations" and the historic names that adorn the walls of the auditorium.

Every month every student was required to "declaim" in his home room, and if he produced a stellar performance, then in the auditorium before the full class. This involved memorizing a poem or a speech, standing up at the front of the class and "declaiming." Edwin Tupper Anthony was the champ in my day, and he went on to become the pastor of the Old Ship Church in Hingham, Massachusetts. It taught us to stand up on our two feet and to speak clearly – I still think it a valuable tradition.

I didn't know much about the names around the top of the auditorium walls while I was a student at Latin School. This was our pantheon of heroes. These were the names of graduates who had made and changed American history. I still remember some of them: Adams, Franklin, Hancock, Paine, Sumner and Putnam! At that stage of life I did not know much about my family history. But I have become more expert since..

Those names honor outstanding graduates of the school. But General Israel Putnam, second in command to George Washington in the American Revolution, went to school in Salem Village. His grand-uncle, John, Jr., in one of the first acts of a Massachusetts legislature in the 1660s, had been "designated to see to the education of the children of Salem Village." So the Putnam name on the Latin School wall honored other Putnams – graduates who became judges or college Presidents, as some did. At least, even in my teens, I took some pride in the fact that I was the only boy in my class of several hundred students whose family name graced the walls of our school.

Two names have been added in this century. "Kennedy" is up there now, presumably for Joseph P. Kennedy – a bona fide graduate. Iffy if he qualifies on the basis of a meritorious life – friendly to Hitler Germany, admirer of Father Coughlin, supporter of Senator Joe McCarthy, on-again-off-again Roosevelt Democrat. I'll give him an "A" – 100 at Boston Latin School! – only for fatherhood. He produced three great sons – Jack, Bobbie and Teddie – a fabulous achievement!

Jack would qualify on the basis of his record as President, but he was not a graduate.

The only other name added to the frieze in this century is "Bernstein" – for Leonard Bernstein, whose lovely music graced our days.

Those were difficult times – the great depression in 1929, the death of my mother in 1931, and the death of my grand-father in 1932. I was lucky to get through Boston Latin School. I was lucky to qualify for a great college.

But I still remember Boston Latin School with fondness.

Chapter 9

CIRCUMNAVIGATION OF NEW ENGLAND

Prior to the magical summer of 1933, nobody had ever pad-dled a canoe or kayak around New England. And to my surprise, nobody has ever done it since!

Pete Knight and I completed nearly two thousand miles in sixty-six days of the summer of 1933, paddling from Burlington on Lake Champlain, Vermont, into the St. Lawrence River and around the Gaspé Peninsula and then New England to New York City. He was a recent graduate of Dartmouth College and I had just gradu-ated from Boston Latin School. I had been accepted as a freshman for the Dartmouth Class of 1937.

"Pete" was Charles Lewis Knight, Jr., of West Roxbury, Massachusetts, the son of the chief of staff of the Forest Hills Hospital and Sadie Knight, who was a leader in the Boston Women's City Club. His brother was John Ellis Knight, about Dartmouth '25, who later became the chief surgeon of the Faulkner Hospital in West Roxbury.

I had met Pete at Camp Waldron on Lake Winnisquam, New Hampshire, in the summer of 1931, when he was the canoe counsellor and I was his assistant. I discovered quickly that he was thoroughly at home on the water, that he was a fierce competitor with unusual upper-body strength and that he liked to wrestle. He especially liked to wrestle when he could win and could force his opponent to "quit."

He could inflict great pain, and I felt it when I was only fifteen years old and still gaining some youthful strength. But it was against my heritage and my training to "quit" and I never did. I can still feel the pain in my arms! When he learned that I would not "quit" in a wrestling match, he thought he could force it on the water.

His idea of constructive after-dinner exercise was to paddle a racing canoe around the lake for the hour before dusk – in racing position on our outside knees and at full speed. Lake Winnisquam is about eight miles long, and a nightly trip along both shores would be about fifteen miles. I was expected to "quit" or drop exhausted into the bottom of the canoe – but I never did!

The next summer, Pete figured that the safest way to get his handsome 14-foot racing canoe back to Boston was to paddle it all the way – about 225 miles. "Want to make the trip with me?"

"Sure." My mother had died recently and my father had moved to Maine. I just had to get back to Boston to finish my final year at Latin School.

We paddled down the Winnipesaukee River, then the full length of the Merrimac River, and then on the ocean from Newburyport through the Annisquam Canal at Gloucester and around Nahant into the Charles River Basin at Boston. Four nights sleeping on the river bank in a single blanket or on the floor of hospitable yacht clubs.

After two summers of being his inexhaustible bow canoe-mate, Pete invited me take part in his wildest dream: "Could you get the summer of 1933 off? I want to paddle around New England in a kayak. My dad and I have designed one, and we are ready to have the builder go to work on it."

Getting permission to spend an entire summer on a canoe trip was something that would require special diplomacy. My father had lost his automobile agency in the depth of the depression, and he would not welcome my forfeiture of a $50. counsellor stipend or the prospect of paying one dollar a day for my food.

"Have him come over to dinner (at the Knight home in

West Roxbury), so that my folks can talk to him." That was a solemn and decisive occasion!

My father and I had a strange relationship at that point. My mother had died a year earlier, and she had made all my career decisions to age 15 – good ones and with my complete accord. My father was not that informed about or sensitive to my ambitions – he was lobbying for me to apply to Bowdoin College and I had no intention of applying anywhere but to Dartmouth! But he liked the outdoors and he was at home on the water himself – he would probably say "Yes."

Dr. and Mrs. Knight explained the details over a sumptuous dinner. They would design the kayak and have it built. They would supply a special tent that would roll up into a one-foot ball, and silk rain-gear that would compress to the size of a fist. Plus charts, a compass, a rifle and a camera. "All we would ask from you is that you provide 'Put' with a dollar a day – which is what we figure it will cost for food."

Sixty dollars (!) was a lot of money to my father in 1933 – especially a lot of money for a 17-year-old boy who should be earning money, not spending it! I am sure that he sensed there was no way he could say "NO." And I don't think he wanted to! I think he took some pride from the fact that I was asked! And I am sure that he concluded it was the kind of adventure that would have excited him in his own youth.

The Knights went ahead with their plans. They invited me to the J. R. Robertson canoe factory – not far from what used to be Norumbega Park in Newton on the banks of the Charles River. Here one man, who had built canoes all his life, was fashioning a kayak according to a design that had never been tried before. It had the shape of an Esquimo kayak, but it was being assembled by traditional canoe construction – canvas over a ribbed wood frame. It was about nineteen feet long and about 30" wide, with cockpits for two men – the rain-jackets would clip over the cockpit holes so that no water could ever enter the interior of the kayak. Watertight under any conditions!

We tried it in May of 1933 with a run from the Boston waterfront out to Boston Light, about ten miles out and another ten miles back. I learned that a 22-year-old man does not get as hungry as a 17-year-old boy. I was starved! And Pete never gave food a very high priority!

After the close of school in June, we were transported to Burlington, Vermont, in Jack Knight's Essex – with the kayak riding right-side up in a specially-constructed cradle on the top of the car. Jack helped us into the water – and we were on our own-for 65 days. For more than one thousand years, Lake Champlain has been the connecting link between the St. Lawrence Valley and the Hudson River, which runs southerly to what is now New York City and the Atlantic Ocean. In the friendly months of summer, it is one of the most idyllic places on earth. Nothing beats a plunge into the hospitable waters of the lake from a friendly ledge of the Hero Islands, warmed by the summer sun.

We paddled north to Rowse's Point and the customs station that guards the locks and the water route into the Richelieu River, which will take us north and into the St. Lawrence. A customs officer yells at us – probably never before having seen a kayak apply for entry into the locks:

"Where you fellahs going?"

I hesitated. If I said, "Boston" – he wouldn't believe me. If I said, "New York City," – he would think I was nuts. And he would probably add that I was heading in the wrong direction – New York City was to the south of us. Cautiously, I replied: "Quebec."

"Go ahead. Good luck to you."

We paddled north on the Richelieu, using the current where we could and stopping for the night along the waterfront of a friendly farming community. We were in a foreign land. We were meeting people who spoke a foreign language! Both were firsts for me.

Three years of French at Boston Latin School had not prepared me for what I was hearing now. The most frequent word was – "mor-ee-al" – with the accent on the last syllable. It was days before I deciphered that they meant "Montreal" – with less of an accent on the last syllable.

And even more difficult for me to figure out was – "boopsy bateau." I recalled that "bateau" was probably "boat," but I was baffled by "boopsy." Gradually it dawned on me that "boopsy" was their French-Canadian contraction of "C'est une bon petit bateau." Translation: "That is a good little boat." Oui, monsieur. Yes, sir!

Our good little boat completed the descent of the Richelieu, and headed out into the quickly widening St. Lawrence. This was ocean-going steamship territory. There were places where one could barely see the distant shore. From the beginning of recorded time, this had been the most important highway into the western world. The explorers of the Great Lakes had come up this route!

Our charts showed us a narrowing as we approached Quebec, and we searched for an isolated beach where we could pitch our tent and spend the night. We had been invited to lunch at the Chateau Frontenac, one of the world's most palatial hotels, by the Jackson brothers. I am not sure how they first heard about us, probably from an article in the newspapers. They were lumber dealers from the Boston area, specializing in the importation of rare woods – such as mahogany from Brazil. They must have been canoeists in their younger days, and they probably were alumni of Dartmouth.

They were most kind to us. We located our base camp in Levis, across from the towering cliffs of Quebec, in the city dump. We dressed in the only white-duck trousers we had stored in our limited space, and headed across the river to the floats along the waterfront of the old town. We climbed the steep roadways to the top of the cliffs – the site that guarded for centuries the main entrance to the interior of the western world. A couple of waterborne vagabonds walked into the exclusive Chateau Frontenac!

"The Jackson brothers, please."

"Right this way. They are expecting you in the dining room."

The dining room of the Chateau Frontenac was like nothing else that I had ever seen – enormous, immaculate, ornate, with a spectacular view of the river far below – winding its way to the sea. And the menu that the Jacksons handed us was even more awesome.

Every item had its individual price. Even a slice of bread! Even a pat of butter! And some quick mathematics told me that were it not for the kindness of the Jacksons, the bill would torpedo my meal budget for the summer!

The only really unpleasant part of the voyage was that paddle across the St. Lawrence River from the luxury of the Chateau Frontenac to the real world of our tent that had been erected in the municipal dump!

The next morning we headed down river, hugging the north shore of the St. Lawrence, and seeing in the distance the plume of Montmorency Falls. Destination: Tadoussac at the mouth of one of the deepest rivers in the world, the Saguenay. Pete was navigator, pilot and helmsman. He steered our craft by a tiny rudder, linked to pedals he could operate with his feet! Mine not to reason why – mine just to provide half the pulling power!

But no complaints. I had learned to have complete confidence in the man pulling his weight behind me. And it never waivered – even though it was tested as we headed for Tadoussac, from the most ancient of times a small fishing village on the east bank of the Saguenay where the powerful river joined the equally powerful St. Lawrence.

Our attention was diverted for a moment by playful white whales, but we had no time or energy for sight-seeing. We were in trouble – caught in cross-currents and cross-winds that turned the sea into a turmoil of "haystacks." Mountains of irregular water at least ten feet high – and we had to cross at least a mile of it to reach the port.

The Saguenay poured the drainage of a whole province in a southerly direction, while the St. Lawrence moved the out-put of the Great Lakes in a northeasterly direction, and the winds were at war with both directions! We stepped up our strokes to full power – yet seemed to make no progress.

I had never been frightened in a canoe or kayak with Pete – I had great confidence in his wisdom and experience. I was not frightened at the mouth of the Saguenay – but I began to wonder if we were attempting the impossible. Maybe there was no way to paddle across this maelstrom. We would not be tipped over, if I out-rigged with my paddle on one side and Pete out-rigged on the other – but could we make any forward progress?

We made it – but I had just as soon not try crossing that stretch of wild water again!

The next day called for crossing the St. Lawrence River, from Tadoussac to Cap Chat (Cape of the Cat). The river at that point is more than thirty miles wide. We would be out of sight of land for the first time. We would be relying completely upon charts and a compass!

Cap Chat would be our first introduction to rural, poverty-stricken fishing ports along the Gaspé Peninsula. But we had something special to look forward to! Pete's Dartmouth classmate, Ben Drew, had reported:

"There is a very pretty girl at the grocery store in Cap Chat. Say hello to her for me."

Despite the fact that Pete and I were both young men with normal instincts, this was kind of an asexual trip. I don't ever recall discussing sex or enjoying a sexual opportunity. Yet we did not mind looking up this recommended girl!

After being out of sight of land for a few hours, we would have been delighted to see anything – anything except water! We were relieved when a thin blue height of land began to appear on the southern horizon. As we paddled closer, the land began to loom larger and it became apparent how Cap Chat received its name. The promontory that protected the little harbor resembled a cat, lying peacefully upon its stomach.

We beached our kayak, and lifted it tenderly onto a somewhat rocky shore, and then headed up the hillside – which appeared to be the natural location of a village store. When we were still a hundred yards away, a scantily-clad girl emerged from the front of the store, ran toward us at full speed and threw her welcoming arms around us. Must be the young lady that Ben Drew had recommended!

She had been watching us since we were a speck on the northern horizon – since we grew into a kind of water-bug with our blades flashing regularly in the summer sun. We were the excitement of the year in a village that had nothing but a small Catholic church with a shiny aluminum roof, a winding dirt road, a few modest houses and some fishing boats.

The favorite joke of the men who could speak English and who were aware of their isolation and their limited possibilities was: "In the summer we fish and f---, and in the winter we don't fish."

But what was ahead of us was not funny. We faced about three hundred miles of paddling to round the Gaspé Peninsula and reach New Brunswick – with towering mountains to the south of us and a river widening to fifty and then to one hundred miles to the north of us. Three hundred miles equalled about ten days of paddling from early morning to late afternoon. And it meant a food supply of non-perishable items, obtainable from the girl at Cap Chat – the last stop before a long voyage.

We ate mostly French bread and cheese for two weeks! I was never so tired of French bread and cheese. When we left Canada, I never wanted to see either of them again!

The towering mountains of Gaspé are a continuation of the Adirondacks, and the Green Mountains of Vermont, and they extend easterly to Newfoundland and beyond. Geologists tell us that a million years ago they were thrust upward by a titanic movement of the earth's tectonic plates. At the furthest east of the peninsula the sea has chopped away at them, producing some of the highest cliffs in the western world.

Day by day we moved northeastward, camping at night on some narrow beach in total desolation. Rain was not uncommon – both day and night. Strangely, I came to regard the rain as friendly. Usually it meant no head winds and no crashing seas to obstruct our progress. It seemed quiet and peaceful in the rain. We never held back because of rain.

Once we rounded the Gaspé Peninsula and headed south at last, we faced the greatest danger of the trip – crossing the Bay Chaleur. The charts showed it was clearly more than thirty miles across at the mouth of the bay. And since we wanted to continue down the Northumberland Strait and along the east coast of New Brunswick, we had to make the jump – and paddle for hours out of sight of land.

No problem in daylight hours and fair weather. But head-winds developed and slowed our progress. We persisted on the southerly course, but the winds delayed us. Land began to emerge from the blue horizon, but darkness began to descend also. No need to panic, but we had to prepare to land upon a strange shore in total darkness.

After paddling steadily for more than twelve hours, any shore was a blessing. So we guided the kayak into shallow water, then carried it above the high water mark, and collapsed on the beach for an all-night sleep. When we woke up in the morning, we discovered that we were in the middle of an abandoned fish-drying camp, and everything we owned was crawling with little white maggots!

But the future was beckoning. The 800-foot cliffs and the formidable St. Lawrence were behind us. We were nearing the friendly coast of New England, and we were excited about the uniqueness of descending the Bay of Fundy. And we had heard that we might encounter a spectacular squadron of flying boats en route from Italy to the World's Fair in Chicago. Dictator Benito Mussolini was flexing his muscles before the world – by sending a flight of planes across the Atlantic for the first time ever.

We encountered them at Shediac, New Brunswick – anchored quietly in the harbor for the night. About twenty of them. Hulls about the size of PT boats. Single wings with a top-mounted propeller and engine. With a tail extension carrying double rudders. Riding our kayak, perhaps the most ancient form of the transportation of man, we surveyed serenely what may have been the most recent and the most modern.

But on to the Bay of Fundy, and our first portage. The city of Moncton sits on the isthmus that separates New Brunswick from Nova Scotia, and it marks the headwaters of perhaps the most unique Bay in the world. It is noteworthy for a rise and fall of tide in excess of forty feet! At the north end of the Bay a "reversing falls" marks the change of tides – water cascading over a ledge northward on the incoming tide and changing direction to head for the open sea when the tide falls. And the incoming tide is heralded by a "bore" – a wall of water about three feet high that marches relentlessly northward twice a day.

We had never encountered a 40-foot tide. We had never seen a harbor front, where the warehouses and piers seemed to be perched half-way to the sky. We had no intention of fighting the incoming tide. We intended to paddle from high tide at Moncton to low tide – as far down the Bay as we could travel in six hours until the "bore" returned.

We rested, provisioned our kayak and then watched the reversing fall – until we could determine slack tide. Then- ready, on your mark, get set – GO!

We sped down the Bay – our usual five knots augmented by about five knots of current. Watching the time, and as the hours passed, watching the growing mud banks and the increasing distances to high ground. We had no intention of lingering in the trickle of water in the center of the Bay at low tide – only to be smashed by an incoming "bore." In due time, we headed for the safety of the high water mark along the banks – slogging through a foot of mud for about half a mile – two weary men towing a 19-foot kayak that was slithering along behind them on a sea of mud!

A barge captain – perched in his bulky craft along the shore line – hailed us: "Hey. You guys. Come over here." He lived on his barge and seemed to have spent his whole life in this strange surrounding.

"Tie up alongside, and come aboard."

We appreciated his hospitality and his expertise. The kayak could sit on the mud and rise with the incoming tide. We needed to clean off, to rest, to eat and then to sleep for one night before descending with the tide once again – this time hopefully to reach Passamaquoddy Bay and the coast of Maine. And his two teen-age girls, who also lived on the barge, were like hand-maidens of the gods!

Down the Bay again with the next retreating tide, past Campobello Island, where Franklin D. Roosevelt contracted polio, through the islands of Passamaquoddy Bay with a careful eye on our charts, and then to the lighthouse at Eastport, Maine – the most easterly point in the United States! Courtesy of the light-house keeper we spent a comfortable night on the spotless floor of this ancient sentinel.

Pete was anxious to reach Deer Isle, only a day's run down the coast of Maine, and the scenic wonderland where his family owned a seaside farm. We could paddle right up to the roadway to the house and we found it without difficulty. This was where my partner had learned much of his seamanship and navigation during his growing-up years.

And he was on good terms with the neighbors, especially the Allen family which during the summers occupied the farm next door. I was unprepared for the warm reception from Mrs.

Allen that overwhelmed us and the bevy of high school boys and girls that swarmed through the house.

We had arrived during preparations for the Number One social event of the summer – a formal ball somewhere on the island. They were awaiting the descent of Mrs. Allen's daughter from the sanctuary of the second floor. We all stood expectantly in the first-floor hall.

When she appeared at the head of the stairs – fancily-clothed for the ball – I almost fainted. She looked like an angel descending from Heaven! Having attended an all-boy high school for four years and having spent the summer on an all-boy voyage, I was unprepared for this reminder of the attractiveness of the other sex. The Queen of the Ball descended the stairs demurely, and I was introduced to Mrs. Allen's daughter – Lucille!

I never forgot her name, but our paths did not cross again until fifteen years later when I began running for public office in Needham, Massachusetts. She became one of my most devoted supporters, but regretfully she had married someone named Remsen!

Pushing westerly down the coast of Maine, we discovered that we were becoming celebrities. Small papers along the coast were beginning to report our progress, and forecast our daily destinations.

We paddled through Eggemoggin Reach and across Penobscot Bay , reaching Rockland during "Homecoming Day" and entering the canoe-tilting contest. The sponsors should have limited it to hometown boys, because Pete was a cat when perched on the gunwales of a canoe and I was expert at maneuvering the craft into a position from which my partner could deliver the knock-out blow. We were like the skilled forester who knows just where to fell the monstrous tree.

We did not want to cause an injury to our opponent when he fell backwards against the middle thwart of his canoe, so we approached almost at a right angle. One punch from Pete's padded pole sent the local yokel flying in an arc into the cold waters of Rockland harbor. We picked up our medals, and continued on down the coast.

Our charts were now very useful. We could tell where we could find a lee shore, where we could avoid troublesome currents, where we could avoid human habitations and where we could find a sandy beach for an easy landing. And rounding one rocky peninsula after another, we often saw small cheering sections waving at us and occasionally we pulled into a lee cove for a proffered cup of coffee.

Lighthouse keepers and yacht clubs were equally kind. They provided clean and safe places to stop for the nights. They sped us on our way southward. We were on familiar territory from Newburyport into Boston – we had paddled this course in 1932 in a 14-foot racing canoe.We rounded Nahant and Winthrop, and paddled into the harbor past Graves Light, and through the Charles River locks into the Basin and the rowing club landing at the Massachusetts Institute of Technology. Dr. Knight was waiting for us, along with Paul V. Craigue, a feature writer for The Boston Globe. A mere four years later I joined Paul on the reportorial staff of the Globe, after graduation from college.

I think now that the Knights had intended to end the round-New England trip at Boston, but we were two weeks ahead of schedule. It was mid-August, and school did not reopen until after Labor Day. Why not continue, and finish up at New York City?

After hardly enough time to go home to Hyde Park and take a bath, we departed the Basin, headed out through the south channel past Boston Light, and then southerly down the coast past Nantasket, Hingham, Scituate, Marshfield, Plymouth where The Mayflower had lain at anchor over the winter of 1620-21 and through the Cape Cod Canal.

Rain or shine, we could clip off the mileage at the regular rate of about thirty miles a day – except for hurricanes. We ran into our first hurricane at Narragansett Bay, and it held us up at the Brenton Reef Coast Guard Station on the eastern shore of the bay.

"Better stay right here for a day or so," the Commander advised. "We don't want to have to pull you out of the bay." We were unable to convince him that our craft was more seaworthy than his – although we believed it!

One day went by while the full intensity of the hurricane hit the southern coast of Connecticut and Rhode Island – then into the second day. We had to watch the days now – if we were to wind up at New York City and still make our college entry dates in early September. We could not spare a full second day. And we watched enviously as the storm winds switched to northeast – the direction that would tail-wind us right along our westerly course.

"We can make it now," Pete advised the Commander.

He gave up restraining us or cautioning us: "We'll watch you from the tower, and we'll notify Point Judith to be on the look-out for you."

"Thanks for everything. We really appreciate your fine hospitality." The Coast Guard eats better than we had any place on the trip – except the Chateau Frontenac!

The waves of Narragansett Bay were the fiercest that I had ever seen – never equalled until I was caught in the North Atlantic in mid-winter on a Liberty ship twelve years later. A good fifteen feet high, the tops whipped horizontally into blistering "horse tails." The troughs so deep we thought we might never see the horizon again. Point Judith over the horizon and due west. But at the tops of the waves, we could feel the diminishing gale blowing us helpfully toward the day's goal.

We made Point Judith on schedule. Rested for the night and then made the Mystic Seaport, and were allowed to sleep on the deck of the old whaler, Charles W. Morgan. It was still afloat in 1933, although I understand it has now been encased in concrete to further extend its historic life.

When we last visited an historic ship, Admiral Donald B.

MacMillan's schooner, Bowdoin, Pete was in favor of a wrestling match on deck, and I was weak enough not to have much to say about it. But I suddenly realized that Pete had given up wrestling – I had reached an equal weight and I had conditioned into equal strength, and there was a good chance I could pin his shoulders in a final defeat!

We paddled westerly down Long Island Sound, into the rushing waters of the East River, through the busy water traffic at the tip of Manhattan Island, and then up the Hudson past the giant ocean liners to the George Washington Bridge. Sitting on the east shore there was the Knickerbocker Canoe Club – and Ernie Reidel, the national champion, was there to greet us. Trip concluded. Off to college.

All this happened sixty-three years ago!

It seems like yesterday!

Chapter 10

DARTMOUTH COLLEGE DAYS (1933-1937)

I love Dartmouth College!

I never applied anywhere else! I never considered any-where else! If the Dartmouth approval letter had not arrived on schedule in April of 1933, I would have been lost and hopeless. And not being prepared for an unfavorable outcome was risky in those days – only one out of eight applicants were accepted – and the risk is even greater today.

But even at age 17, I seemed to be certain that I was sailing under a lucky star, and setting my course to Dartmouth was the best decision that I ever made. I credit some distinguished alumni that I had the good fortune to meet in my youth.

The Reverend Sidney Lovett of Mount Vernon Church in Boston, a founder of my boys' camp, had seen me hit a home-run when his Yankee pitcher had one-hit my camp team, and he was en-route to becoming the Chaplain of Yale University. Dartmouth was sufficiently aware of his good works to award him an honorary degree in 1937.

The Reverend Everett Moore Baker, the Dartmouth '25 director of my camp, had awarded me the coveted "Loyalty Medal." "Uncle Ev" went on to become the Dean of Students at the Massachusetts Institute of Technology, so his recommendation would have carried great weight at Dartmouth. And Pete Knight of the Class of 1932 was my favorite canoe mate. Those recom-mendors must have won me considerable support in the

Admissions Office.

And even earlier, my home town of Hyde Park thought well of Dartmouth, because of Jerry Harlow and Jack Manchester, members of the class of 1932. Jerry's sister, Betsy, was the sweetest young lady in my dancing class, and Jack's brother, Freddie, was one of my favorite hockey buddies. We used to play on the oily frozen surface of the Neponset River.

Before his death in 1996 at Kendal of Hanover, Jack and I used to reminisce about our hockey days:

"Remember the time that you and Freddie brought your scrub team up to play us at New Hampton Academy?"

I remembered the game – on an outdoor rink in bitter cold weather: "I think we beat you. We gave you more than you bargained for."

Jack went on to a fine career at Dartmouth, and became a kind of life-long godfather of Dartmouth hockey.

After Labor Day in September of 1933, my father made the four-hour drive from Boston to Hanover, New Hampshire, over the two-lane highways of those times. There may have been one remaining stretch of dirt road – as we cut over the hills northwest of Concord to the remote town of Potter Place. I had spent many summers in New Hampshire, but had never experienced the Granite State in any other season. And now there was a touch of fall in the air, and the hint of autumnal colors in the trees. I had never seen the Dartmouth campus – but as we topped the hill en route from Lebanon to the Hanover plain, there was the tower of Baker Library before me – and the ageless buildings of my college. For me – then and now – this was and is my Shangri-La!

We parked my grandfather's $1,000. at the Dartmouth National Bank, in the first checking account that I ever had, and proceeded to College Hall (now named for my classmate, Charlie Collis). Second floor, top of the stairs, next to the John – conveniently located at the center of the campus and next to Freshman Commons where I labored during every one of my four years at the college.

When an alumnus has been out of college for nearly sixty years, the undergraduate years are vivid memories – flashbacks to a magic time: the first walk around the campus in a freshman "beanie," the football games in the stadium, the smorgasbord of learning – about psychology and evolution and English literature – skating on Occum Pond in sub -zero temperatures, a date with a "townie" girl and not even kissing her! And Alan Bryant of my class singing a solo with the Dartmouth Glee Club on the steps of Dartmouth Hall on a spring evening, – his rich, tenor voice caressing each meaningful word of "Dartmouth Undying."

Only in recent years have I had an opportunity to spend entire summers in Hanover, New Hampshire, and my reactions are best expressed in my poem – Lovely Land:

> Lakes and mountains
> Trees and sky
> To lovely lands
> Returned am I.
>
> Scenes of boyhood
> Thoughts of man -
> Return as often
> As one can.
>
> Sing like song-birds
> Shout the joy
> Voice the pleasures
> Of a boy!

Still the most striking thing about the Dartmouth campus is the arboreal splendor – the elms and the maples that have been nurtured for centuries in sightly places. The giant elm that was in front of College Hall in 1933 is still there – and its girth has grown from about six feet to nearer ten feet. Time and money and employee dedication and scientific progress have staved off some of the devastation of the Dutch elm disease – until now a variety has been discovered and cultivated that has some ability to resist the scourge.

I can't think of any other place in New England where trees and buildings have been melded into a more impressive cathedral for learning. In 1995, the old trees moved me to this poem:

> Who saved the elms?
> Who saved these kingly trees?
> Who kept them spiking to the sky?
> Who made sure they did not die?
>
> Their graceful branches sheltered me
> In freshman days of long ago,
> They witnessed scenes of ice and snow,
> They blessed the years of Dartmouth Row.
>
> This tree was old when I was young,
> Its age is now notched up a rung.
> Who saved this master of the sky?
> Who made sure they did not die?

My Dartmouth Class of 1937 numbered around 500 boys – no girls then! Many of them were my friends in college and many of them have remained my friends through all the years. And many have lived important lives!

Dr. C. Everett Koop ("Chick" in college days and "Chick" to us still!) was appointed Surgeon General by President Reagan, and has become an important spokesman for sounder health policies.

Professor Russell Stearns, whom I remember waiting on tables in Freshman Commons, was a recent President of the American Society of Civil Engineers.

Charles Collis has been one of the college's all-time most

generous benefactors.

J. Wilcox Brown has never wavered in his devotion to the natural beauties of his State of New Hampshire and to enlightened leadership in New Hampshire politics.

William Rotch was the fifth generation of his family to own and edit the Milford, New Hampshire, Cabinet.

Francis Fenn and A. Benedict Doran have been tireless fund-raisers for the college.

And Thomas J . McIntyre of our Dartmouth Class of 1937 went from ringing doorbells for Franklin D. Roosevelt in the Upper Connecticut Valley in 1936 to the United States Senate – in our book the best Senator from New Hampshire in this half century.

Many of my classmates have been important leaders in their home communities. They exemplify the purpose of the college – to educate young people so they can lead useful lives. Most of them are active, concerned and courageous – I am proud of them!

But what plucks at the heartstrings when an alumnus returns to Hanover are the unchanging sights – only at Dartmouth has time stood still for sixty years, at least as to the physical surroundings. I can walk down the path to the Ledyard Canoe Club on the east bank of the Connecticut River, and find the clubhouse looking exactly as it did in my student days. I won the college canoe championship right there in my freshman year. I took the photos of at least two girl friends right on that front porch. I sat there and overheard the debate over who would be our officers in my senior year.

And I was summer director there in 1934. But there has been one important change – the summer director in 1996 was from London! – a girl named Mary. Lithe and beautiful and competent!

The buildings and the scenery may be largely unchanged over the centuries, but in this intellectual environment one must be prepared for meetings and contacts that may blow your mind!

President David McLaughlin appointed me to the Board of Visitors of the Tucker Foundation, a social service/leadership program of the college, and at the next meeting I introduced myself to a handsome male from about the class of '55.

"And you are?"

"Marshall Meyer."

"What do you do?"

"I am a Rabbi. Now in New York, but I spent most of my adult life in Argentina."

I was stunned. I had just read the autobiography of Jacobo Timmermann, the editor of the Buenos Aires La Prensa, who was arrested, imprisoned and tortured by the military junta that ruled Argentina through the 1970s and before.

"You were the Rabbi of Jacobo Timmermann?" My question must have been one of both awe and worship.

"Yes."

"You led the mother marches for the 'disappeared ones'?"

"Yes."

I never was prouder of my college, of the Tucker Foundation and of President Freedman, who had discovered Rabbi Marshall Meyer and appointed him to our Board.

Rabbi Meyer had risked his life to visit Jacobo Timmerman in a Buenos Aires jail. He had lobbied and agitated for his release. And he had led the mothers of young men who had "disappeared" in regular marches on a picket line at the Presidential palace. The continual agitation eventually brought down the government.

Investigations many years later disclosed that the "disappeared ones" were arrested by the junta police, bound or shackled, placed aboard a military cargo plane and then pushed out the door when the plane was far out over the South Atlantic.

Later the College named Rabbi Meyer a "Montgomery Fellow," the highest honor for a visiting scholar, and he gave his own epitaph in a lecture in Dartmouth Hall on October 17, 1991 –

fortunately, preserved on video. He titled it: "Why and How To Be An Activist."

He was a chain smoker, and as a result, he died an untimely death. He was the bravest alumnus that I ever knew. I was honored to be his friend!

My own epitaph will not be as important, but I take a quiet pride in the fact that I have two paintings in the permanent collection of Dartmouth College, at least two books in the collection of Baker Library and some 16 mm. sound/color motion pictures in the archives of the Dartmouth Film Society. (Olympic canoeing coach Jay Evans adds: "and that famous West River painting that hangs over the canoe club fireplace, as well as two famous paddles.")

We used to have an old college cheer that went: "Gimme a D... Gimme an A... Gimme an R... Gimme a T... etc." – until we spelled out "Dartmouth," in the years when college cheering was much better than it is now.

For me, I suggest: "Gimme a V" – for versatility. Grade me "A" for versatility! Dartmouth College teaches that subject also!

Chapter 11

"HOW'S THE OLD GLOBE?"

The President of the United States looked up at me with his famous smile, and asked: "How's the old Globe?"

FDR was at his desk in the Oval Office of the White House at the conclusion of one of his famous press conferences. David K. Niles took me forward to make the introduction:

"Putnam is with the Boston Globe, Mr. President. He ran our Independents for Roosevelt and Wallace in Massachusetts last fall."

This was in 1941 just after we had elected the President to his third term – the only President ever to be elected to three terms. I knew Dave not only as one of the six "anonymous Administrative Assistants" then allowed to the President by Congress, but as the Executive Director of Ford Hall Forum in Boston, where I volunteered my public relations assistance.

Press conferences were very different in those days, and so was the staffing of the White House. Attendance at the conference ran around thirty, mostly regular Washington correspondents. Questions were always polite and respectful, and the President was always both knowledgeable and at ease. No President ever responded to the media more skillfully. A conference always ended peacefully: "Thank you, Mr. President."

FDR had a genuine interest in The Boston Globe because he had been a stringer for our paper during his student days at Harvard College. And I had a warm interest in him, because his

National Youth Administration made it possible for me to finish my four years at Dartmouth College. The $40. per month check came regularly for my forty hours of labor in the college library.

I was lucky to make it to the Globe after my graduation from Dartmouth in 1937. The Great Depression had not yet disappeared over the far horizon, and jobs of any kind were still scarce. Having majored in English and being interested in writing, my mind was made up in favor of journalism – but for whom? I tried first The Boston Herald – which was my family newspaper.

They had a nice, new building at 80 Mason street in downtown Boston, and I found my way up to the office of the editor, Robert Choate. He sat behind a big, mahogany desk, was of medium build and had close cropped hair and he appeared to me sort of like a grumpy Marine officer. Or perhaps the great stone face up in the White Mountains, because I don't remember him saying anything.

After I said what I could, he dismissed me: "We don't have anything at the present time. If anything develops, we will get in touch with you." I concluded that Hell would freeze over before that happened.

Justice was done four years later when I was about to be introduced to Mr. Choate at an important cocktail party. My Globe column was then the most widely read newspaper feature in New England. "No need to introduce me," I responded. "I applied to Mr. Choate for a job a few years ago, and he didn't hire me."

The Herald editor was much more affable now, and was kind enough to say: "Dumbest mistake I ever made."

I went to the Globe with more effective credentials, a letter to City Editor George Dimond from the Reverend Ralph Rowse, the Superintendent of the City Missionary Society – the social service arm of the Congregational churches in the Boston area. "Uncle Ralph" knew me from summer camp, and I had labored with him to construct much of the roadway that made it possible for a supply truck to reach us. I was confident that he had some good things to say in the reference letter that he offered me.

"Mr. Rowse suggested that I talk with you, and that I deliver this letter from him," I said to Mr. Dimond, introducing myself.

He was nearing retirement age – big, genial, a shock of snow-white hair. He reminded me of Santa Claus. He was sitting in front of a roll top desk in a corner of the City Room, surrounded by a clutter of paper in all stages of usefulness. But most importantly, he was kindly and he seemed genuinely interested in my welfare. He read Mr. Rowse's letter carefully.

"He says some nice things about you." I was not surprised. "We don't have anything right now. But I will check around and see what we can do. Don't be discouraged. Keep in touch."

I did keep in touch, but in the meantime, I discovered that the Hyde Park Gazette, a weekly, would take me on as a reporter at $10. per week! And I could dig up the stories, write them exactly as they would appear, add the headlines, and proofread the copy. Plus – I would be needed on Thursdays to help get the run off the flatbed press. And I could write my own byline column. What more could an ambitious young journalist ask? A chance at The Boston Globe!

It came in the winter of 1938. Lucien Thayer called – the successor to George Dimond: "We can use you as a copy boy."

"Fine."

"The pay will be $15. per week." No problem. What could I say? That was a 50 per cent raise.

"You will work the night shift – 5 p.m. until 2 a.m."

"Yes, sir.."

I spent eleven years with the Globe – with two and a half years out for Naval officer service in World War 2. They were exciting times. I interviewed Cabinet officers, the Vice President, the Governors, Ambassador Joseph Kennedy, and I spoke on the same platform with a young Kennedy who decided to run for Congress in 1946 – John F. Kennedy.

My Victory Forum in the early 1940s and the successor, The Veterans Forum, in the postwar years filled a need for accurate and prompt information on massive government programs that touched the lives of everyone. Readers liked the short questions and the pithy answers. The Veterans Administration came to dread reading about their misdeeds in the Globe column. I would run some veteran's agonizing trouble, and then sign only his claim number. The VA could identify the problem, and usually could correct the matter within twenty-four hours. I still meet doctors who thank me for running their complaint. "I could not have stayed in med school, if you had not bombed my check out of them."

But things were not all that peaceful and promising on the domestic front. I had married Betty Mason of Hyde Park in 1939. Our parents had taken us by the hand in 1921 to the same kindergarten, at the same time, and at the same church. And the wife of our clergyman kept urging us to marry only someone from our own church. I am not sure that Jesus would have supported that advice.

We produced three wonderful daughters – Wendy (1941), Ann (1944) and Judith (1947). I stayed with the marriage until 1966, and provided the wherewithal to send all three children through four years of college. But our needs and ambitions were never the same – and my in-laws never became accustomed to a son-in-law who thought well of Roosevelt and neither did my wife.

A career in elective office in Massachusetts and appointive office in Washington is not very compatible with a traditional marriage. Families get what is left after the compelling demands of the political career. I can see it now more clearly from Betty's point of view:

What do you do with a husband who resigns the best newspaper job in New England to run for an elective office that pays $2,000. per year? At a time when you have three young children.

What do you do when he worsens the situation by

enrolling in law school, instead of going out and earning some supplementary income?

And then this relentless crusader decides to run for Congress against an incumbent millionaire – with only $6,000. available in his campaign fund!

The struggle between my political aspirations and domestic bliss continued unabated from 1948 to 1966. By then my hopes of going to Congress had been dashed. The children had been cared for through their majority. I ended the marriage.

Those middle years were the most difficult of my life, which is not unique. I suspect they are for almost everyone. Looking backward, would I have juggled the priorities differently? I don't think so. Our country could still use the kind of Congressman that I would have been.

I still have fond memories of my years with The Boston Globe – 1938 to 1949. I am grateful to William O. Taylor, Davis Taylor and John I. Taylor – the then owners of the Globe – for their confidence in me. I was only in my 20s during most of those years.

They boosted me to the top of the editorial staff, and backed my column that became the most widely read in New England. They even let me film and narrate Globe Headlines of 1949, which is now in the archives of the Dartmouth Film Society – with priceless shots of Winston Churchill, Jawarhalal Nehru, Speaker John McCormack, John F. Kennedy, Bernard Baruch, Ted Williams and Clarence DeMar.

Laurence L. Winship edited the Globe back then. He made the decisions that gave me exciting opportunities at an early stage of my life. Honor to his memory – a great editor.

Back in the 1940s, no-one would have predicted that the Boston Globe would be the chief survivor of the battles of the Boston newspapers. Gone are the Transcript, the American and the Post. And the Herald is only a shadow of its former self.

I rejoice that for better than a decade I had a small part in this fortunate result.

"HALF AND HALF"
MARION, MASS.
TEL: MARION 416

Dear Harold:

Many thanks for your
note. Youre always done
a fine job for the Globe
and "Veterans Forum" wont
be the same without your
great interest.

I, too, hope our paths
will cross often and I
admire anyone beginning
the fight in politics and
the law.

Best of luck
Dave Taylor

1948 - Note from publisher Davis Taylor as author resigns as
Boston Globe columnist to become a State Representative.

Chapter 12

FRANKLIN D. ROOSEVELT
1882 – 1945

ELEANOR ROOSEVELT
1884 – 1962

No married couple in the twentieth century had such an impact upon American life – and upon world history – as Franklin and Eleanor Roosevelt.

Once a week I talk history to a 5th grade class at a local elementary school, and when I tell them about a personal experience with President or Mrs. Roosevelt, they look at me with awe!

Not with disbelief – because they know that I would not tell them an untruth. But they view me as the last survivor of a bygone age…They find it hard to comprehend that I was around and alert more than forty years before they were born.

I grew up in a Republican family. I was twelve years old when Al Smith was the Democratic candidate for President against Herbert Hoover in 1928. A Sunday paper carried a full page photograph of Governor Smith, and I recall being shocked when a family friend handed it to my father and recommended that it be used for toilet paper!

Republicans were cocky in those flamboyant days before the Great Depresssion. They came down to earth – and cruel reality – after the 1929 collapse of the stock market, and the calamitous years of 1930 and 1931. Governor Franklin D. Roosevelt of New York swept into the Presidency in a landslide in 1932, and the

United States and the world were changed forever.

During my four years at Dartmouth College in Hanover, New Hampshire, (1933-1937), I learned that who occupied the White House made a big difference to me personally. Only vaguely did I understand the sweeping reforms being recommended by Roosevelt and being passed by Congress, but the National Youth Administration was close and personal.

It paid me $40. per month to preserve ancient leather books in the Baker Library and to index the art books in Carpenter Hall. That subsistence allowance kept me in college, and the exhortations of my President seemed to make it all worthwhile.

In fireside chats and press conferences, the President urged young people to complete their educations – keeping them off the job market for a few years and hopefully making them more useful citizens for the rest of their lives.

When I went to The Boston Globe in 1938, it was not difficult for me to join most of the other young reporters in supporting the "New Deal." I maintained the technical independence of a fair reporter, but my private sympathies were with President Roosevelt.

My boyhood Congressman, John W. McCormack of South Boston, became the Majority Floor Leader and championed the Roosevelt legislative program. Thomas H. Eliot, a brilliant young Harvard lawyer, went to Washington and wrote much of the Social Security Act.

Professor Felix Frankfurter at Harvard Law School was sending a stream of outstanding graduates to Washington to firm up a creative legislative program.
The Holmes and Brandeis Supreme Court dissents of the 1920s became the law of the land.

And the Roosevelt lieutenants came through Boston regularly – Harry Hopkins, Harold Ickes, Henry Wallace, and Joseph E. Davies, who sent me an autographed copy of his thoughtful book, "Mission to Moscow."

All of these leaders I met through reporter assignments at The Boston Globe, but they developed into friendships often through the intercessions of David K. Niles, the executive director of Ford Hall Forum. At the end of the 30s, overwhelmed by White House duties, President Roosevelt asked Congress to please give him sufficient money for "six anonymous administrative assistants." Dave became one of the six.

They kept out of the press and off the air waves, and they never wrote any books disclosing the intimate details of the White House operation. They quietly achieved great things. Dave was the President's liaison with the Jewish community, and he had an important hand in the creation of the State of Israel, the founding of Brandeis University and the success of the Presidential campaigns of 1940 and 1944.

Dave used to take the sleeper from Washington to Boston on Friday evenings, spend all day Saturday and Sunday in Boston, and then after the Sunday night Forum was underway, take the sleeper back to Washington. Every Saturday afternoon, he would be at his Forum office in the Little Building, at the corner of Boylston and Tremont streets in Boston, and he would spend most of it listening to the Metropolitan Opera, then only on radio.

While he relaxed, Herbert Black of The Boston Globe and I would grind out the press releases for the program coming up on the following week-end. Dave's contacts enabled him to book the top speakers from around the world: Norman Thomas, Bertrand Russell, W.E.B. DuBois, Rabbi Stephen Wise, Rev. John Haynes Holmes, and Roger Baldwin, the founder of the American Civil Liberties Union. The lines of people anxious to hear them often stretched around the block on Sunday evenings. The format became famous, and the speakers usually enjoyed it as much as the audience: the speaker was given one hour from 8 to 9 p.m. to speak his (or her) piece, and then the audience could fire any questions that were pertinent for the final hour.

Some the exchanges became hot and heavy. I remember

one evening when Rabbi Wise blasted the press – I thought very unfairly – and I challenged his position with a few well-chosen remarks. At least I thought they were well- chosen.

The next day my editor, Laurence L. Winship, called me into his office to tell me: "Reporters should be seen, but not heard."

So I never jumped to my feet in Ford Hall Forum again, but I became more deeply involved in national politics. Dave invited me to head the Massachusetts Independents for Roosevelt and Wallace in the 1940 campaign, when FDR campaigned for his third term. This seemed to preserve the independence that I thought proper for a political reporter, so I accepted.

I had interviewed Henry Wallace more than once, and liked his sincere concern for the public good. He was courageous and far-sighted, qualities that can get your head shot off these days, and were not always successful even in New Deal days. And as a reporter I had often sent along to Harold Ickes some ideas or words that I thought he could put to good use.

Today they call them "sound bites" when they are exploded on television. They were just as effective in the press in New Deal days, and nobody could light the fuses better than Harold Ickes – ostensibly the Secretary of the Interior, but actually President Roosevelt's hatchet man on all fronts.

Every President needs a Lieutenant who can cut the legs off an opponent with less than one sentence. Roosevelt was pretty good himself: "Now they are even attacking my little dog, Fala," and who wants to turn the country back to the firm of "Martin, Barton and Fish?" But nobody ever equalled Ickes.

When he left the Boston City Club one day in the company of Boston attorney Larue Brown, I heard him say about me: "That fellow is a live wire." Nicest thing anyone ever said about me! I felt the same way about him!

Fifty years later when I watch a President struggle in deep trouble, I can't help thinking: "He needs someone like the 1940 Harold Ickes."

President Roosevelt wound up his 1940 campaign for a third term at The Boston Garden on the night before the Tuesday election. After the formal speech at the Garden, during which he promised that he would not draft American boys for a foreign war, he made an unheralded trip to the G & G Delicatessen on Blue Hill Avenue in the Dorchester section of Boston – the center of Jewish life in a crucial state. Dave Niles must have arranged that unscheduled stop. I remember the open limousine coming up Blue Hill Avenue, the President remaining in the car, but his powerful and confident voice booming out over thousands of people packed into the street as far as we could see.

We had just begun to hear of the Nazi atrocities against Jews. Our audience was more intimately related to them. The President left no doubt that the United States – under his leadership – would be the champion of human rights, whatever the cost.

When we departed for our homes that night and the President left to be at Hyde Park on election day as usual, none of us doubted that history would be made in November of 1940 by the election of a President for a third term.

* * * * *

Things were comfortably different in those days. Cabinet officers came and went in Boston with no secret service and no caravans of limousines. I can remember them walking across the streets on Beacon Hill to go to lunch with local leaders.

Even Mrs. Roosevelt came to town – even when she was First Lady – with little fanfare. On a Saturday afternoon in 1943, Dave Niles tapped me on the shoulder while I was typing away on a press release for Ford Hall Forum:

"Will you go down to the South Station and pick up Eleanor?"

The First Lady was travelling by regular coach, carrying only a small "Boston bag" for the clothes she would need for a

Sunday appearance at the Forum. Regular folks – gracious lady. I drove her to her hotel – no entourage, no police escort, so secret service!

No-one suspected at that time that all was not love and kisses in the Roosevelt marriage. "No Ordinary Time" by Doris Kearns Goodwin makes clear that Franklin and Eleanor had become accustomed to an unusual marriage – one that looked good to the public but which hid many agonies in their personal lives.

Today the hint of "another woman" is enough to torpedo any political campaign. Yet FDR maintained close relationships for many years with Missy LeHand, Lucy Mercer Rutherfurd and Crown Princess Martha of Norway. Some lived or visited in the adjacent bedroom in the White House! Lucy was with the President in Warm Springs when he died!

Yet there was no speculation at the time as to the physical capacity of a man who was paralyzed from the waist down. If he retained normal appreciation of fine women, the attitude then and now seems to have been – good luck to him!

I do not recall any interest in or speculation about the sex life of President Roosevelt. How times have changed? Changed for the worse – less interest in the great public issues that shape the destinies of nations and more interest in the personal foibles that beset most of us!

Mrs. Goodwin in her 1994 book touches upon one relationship that did attract our attention in the 1940s – the curious affinity between FDR and his rival for the Presidency in 1940 – Wendell Willkie.

Willkie was an utility company executive advanced by the Republican Party to block a third term. He had come to public attention as the leading opponent of the transformation of the South by the Tennessee Valley Authority – a massive public works program combining cheap power, soil conservation, recreational facilities and job creation.

Willkie was against it! But Willkie was eloquent and he was handsome. He made a good public appearance, and he talked much sense. In an era of narrow partisanship, he seemed broadminded. These qualities were not lost upon the President!

Mrs. Goodwin has discoverered that the White House visitor logs of early 1944 show that Wendell Willkie attended an unheralded meeting with the President in his private quarters, and it lasted throughout a long evening. What did they talk about?

Willkie had toured some foreign countries after his 1940 defeat, and had spoken constructively of his country and his President. He had written a remarkable book entitled "One World," which set the tone for non-partisan approval of The United Nations. Roosevelt and Willkie through the war years seemed to be travelling down the same road.

The author of "No Ordinary Time" suggests that they were talking frankly about a fourth term for FDR. She indicates they might have been considering their personal dream ticket! – Democrat Roosevelt for President and Republican Willkie for Vice President!

They might have been joking, because Roosevelt was exasperated with the failure of many southern Democrats to support both his peacetime and his wartime goals. And Willkie might have gone along with the wild idea with considerable enthusiasm – because he had had his fill with right-wing Republicans and their failure to see the urgency of the war effort and the global opportunities within the coming peace.

They might have secretly enjoyed the wishful thinking. They might have boldly believed that the peace deserved a Third Party – dedicated to the needs of a new and more united world. They surely must have chuckled over the consternation that a Roosevelt-Willkie ticket would have provoked in 1944.

I can offer only some testimony from Speaker Joseph W. Martin, Jr. of Massachusetts, who managed Willkie's Presidential campaign in 1940. When the Speaker lay ill in the Bethesda Naval

Hospital in the 1960s, knowing that life for him was nearing its end and still wistful about the glory days of his long career, his thoughts went back to the Willkie campaign. He leaned toward me and said:

"Willkie was the best leader that the Republicans ever had."

* * * * * * *

During the maneuvering to continue the leadership of FDR during World War 2 and to achieve the almost impossible task of winning a precedent-shattering fourth term, I was at sea – as a Navy gunnery officer on an armed merchant ship.

We had been sent down the east coast of South America, through the Strait of Magellan, up the Chilean inside passage and into Valparaiso. We were returning to the United States via the Panama Canal while the Democratic convention was in progress at Chicago. I was out of touch with the furious internal struggle over who would run with the President as his Vice Presidential candidate.

I had interviewed Vice President Henry A. Wallace (1940-1944) several times, and always regarded him as capable, honest and forthright. He came from a mid-western farm family long appreciated for its dedication to public service.

The electorate and I did not regard him as particularly controversial during Roosevelt's third term. The President seemed to like him, and we expected the top positions on the Democratic ticket to proceed into the 1944 elections unchanged.

But we reckoned without the strength of the conservative opposition within the Democratic party. Many of the leaders had never been happy with the New Deal, and they did not want to see it perpetuated and made even more liberal by Henry A. Wallace. And they had reason to believe that FDR would die early in his fourth term. The 1944 Vice Presidential nominee was almost certain to become President in 1945 or 1946 – and the insiders pre-ferred Senator Harry Truman.

The convention went for Truman. President Roosevelt was too old, too tired and too ill to fight against the removal of Wallace. He accepted the substitution of Truman – although my guess is that his personal choice was still Wallace.

Word of the last minute shift in Vice Presidential nominees came to me via ship radio, and I sat down and wrote my condo-lences to the loser – Henry A. Wallace.

I still have and prize his reply – dated August 14, 1944 – about one month after his removal from the Roosevelt fourth term ticket:

"It is very encouraging to receive a letter like yours...Somehow I think time will demonstrate that the liberal cause has been strengthened by what happened at Chicago."

Didn't work out that way!

OFFICE OF THE VICE PRESIDENT

WASHINGTON

August 14, 1944

Ensign Harold Putnam, USNR
S. S. West Keene
c/o Fleet Post Office
New York City

Dear Mr. Putnam:

It is very encouraging to
receive a letter like yours. Somehow
I think time will demonstrate that the
liberal cause has been strengthened by
what happened at Chicago.

Sincerely yours,

H A Wallace

H. A. Wallace

1944 - This letter from Vice President Henry A. Wallace was written just a few
weeks after an ill President Roosevelt and the Democratic Party ditched
him in favor of Harry Truman, whose Vice Presidential nomination was
sure to lead to the Presidency during the FDR fourth term.

Chapter 13

SACCO AND VANZETTI

Sacco and Vanzetti were electrocuted in Massachusetts in 1927.

Even at the age of eleven, I was old enough to realize that something monumental was happening.

The most notorious murder case of the 20th century in New England involved Nicola Sacco (1891-1927) and Bartolomeo Vanzetti (1888 -1927), a shoe worker and a poor fish peddler. They were condemned to death for a crime that many people were convinced they did not commit.

Although the events occurred in the 1920s, the case remained infamous throughout the century, probably for two reasons:

1.   It was remembered as a shocking miscarriage of justice – involving "the best people," and

2.   It uncovered a deep-seated prejudice against foreigners – and especially against the swelling tide of Italian immigrants.

The murder occurred in 1924, and the trial dragged on until the execution in 1927, involving both a zealous prosecution and a stubborn defense.

The whole Commonwealth of Massachusetts seemed to have been involved in the case, including indirectly me – then a 9 to 12-year-old boy. I remember the furor. I remember the anger. And as I grew older, I remembered the prejudice.

Even the whole world got into the clamor, Sacco and Vanzetti finding more sympathy in foreign lands than in their adopted home. Reporting on the fate of his pencil concession in the Soviet Union, Dr. Armand Hammer has written of visiting his enterprise after being kept away during the decades of the Stalin rule. He found that the company had been renamed "The Sacco and Vanzetti Pencil Factory." The murder occurred in Braintree, about twelve miles southwest of Boston, and the case was tried in Dedham, the county seat adjacent to Hyde Park, where I grew up in the 1920s. Thirty years later I tried my first case to a jury in the same courtroom in which Sacco and Vanzetti had battled unsuccessfully for their lives.

The county prosecutor was Frederick Katzman, also counsel for the Hyde Park Savings Bank where I deposited my boyhood nickels and dimes. I recall hearing about his unrelenting role.

The attorneys for the defense included Herbert Ehrman of Brookline, whose wife I met at the State House in 1949 where she lobbied patiently for many years to outlaw the death penalty in Massachusetts.

Through the decades of the 1940s and 1950s, I don't remember ever meeting anyone who was proud of the conviction and the electrocution. On the other hand, the defenders of Sacco and Vanzetti were legion. Their numbers and their influence grew with the passage of the years. As late as 1988, after a lifetime of authoritative reporting for The Boston Globe, Charles Whipple reported that he was satisfied that the Boston Police switched murder weapons to pin the blame on Sacco and Vanzetti.

Those responsible for the conviction dropped from public office, and sank into obscurity. Those who defended Sacco and Vanzetti advanced in professional standing and in public service. Justice seems to have been done finally – but too late to save the lives of the poor fish peddler and the obscure shoe worker.

Leading the clamor for conviction and electrocution were Governor Alvin T. Fuller and Harvard President Charles W. Eliot.

When they dropped from positions of influence, a few dedicated women kept alive the revulsion against bigotry and injustice in the criminal system.

I met some of them in the 1940s at the Ford Hall Forum and at the Community Church of Boston, both of which I covered for several years as a reporter for The Boston Globe. Dorothy Brown, Jessica Dewey, Gertrude Winslow, Attorney Gael Mahony's mother and Mrs. Arthur Rotch. Many of those women had been suffragettes in the 1910s, and upon the granting of the vote, they had progressed to the founding of the Women's City Club, the launching of the League of Women Voters, and they were supporters of the abolition of the death penalty.

My recollection is that Mrs. Winslow, a kindly, dedicated, courageous lady who bore one of the oldest names in the Massachusetts Bay Colony, visited Sacco and Vanzetti frequently in the final years of their hopeless incarceration. She and others like her were never convinced of their guilt; and the ladies were appalled at the ferocity and the recklessness of the criminal justice system.

The now famous letter from Bartolomeo Vanzetti, the accused fish-peddler, written in his cell during his final days, was, I believe, smuggled out of the prison by Gertrude Winslow, and was made public for posterity:

"If it had not been for this thing, I might have lived out my life talking at street-corners to scorning men. I might have died unmarked, unknown, a failure.

"Now we are not a failure. This is our career and our triumph. Never in our full life could we hope to do such work for tolerance, for justice, for man's understanding of man, as now we do by accident.

"Our words – our lives – our pain: nothing! The taking of our lives – lives of a good shoe-maker and a poor fish-peddler – all! That last moment belongs to us – that agony is our triumph." Vanzetti's letter to his son. April 9, 1927.

His final words were found on a tablet in his cell after the electrocution:

"There is nothing, nowhere, neither on earth nor in the heavens that can make the true untrue or the untrue true."

Wherever one turned in Boston in the 1930s and the 1940s, a concerned citizen would encounter someone who had had a leading role in the Sacco-Vanzetti Defense Committee. When I became editor of the American Newspaper Guild's Boston news letter around 1940, the organizer explained:

"You'll have to take the copy down to Aldino Felicani. He runs the Excelsior Press down near the Boston Garden (for many years the home of the Boston Celtics!). He's a sweet guy, and he will give you all the help you need. He was Treasurer of the Sacco-Vanzetti Defense Committee."

To my generation of journalists, Aldino was a legendary figure – tall, strong, determined, fiercely independent, and dedicated to the accuracy and the power of the printed word. Also, he was deeply hurt and resentful that the all-powerful state had taken his friends from him by what he felt was an abuse of authority.

Aldino was probably a bit of an anarchist, as were and are many educated Italians. Come to think of it he had probably known Benito Mussolini – unfavorably. Since the days of ancient Rome, Italy never seemed to have had an orderly government, yet it made spectacular advances in the arts and the sciences on the wings of some rather unique free spirits.

I imagined that Aldino was very much like Sacco and Vanzetti – sort of working-man intellectuals who had never discovered many good reasons to love governments, but who found it easy to love people – to love humanity.

I wish now that I had discussed the Sacco and Vanzetti case at length with Aldino. I had many occasions to do so, as we prepared the Newspaper Guild copy for the press. Yet, I had the feeling that this physically and intellectually powerful man preferred to keep his bitterness to himself, preferred to nurture his burning resentment – while laboring with rare dedication for a society in which such horrors as the electric chair and oppression by the state would be outlawed.

Another who labored mightily to produce some good from years of dark despair was Mrs. Herbert Ehrman of Brookline, Massachusetts, who was the first lobbyist I met at the State House as a new legislator in 1949. She was continuing her perennial effort to outlaw capital punishment, a cause that became her life's work when her attorney/husband failed in his valiant effort to save Sacco and Vanzetti from the chair in 1927.

"I hope you will support our effort to end capital punishment," Mrs. Ehrman said to me in the corridor of the State House in 1949. She was diminutive, persistent, eloquent and determined. I found it easy to agree with her position. No evidence had ever been produced to prove that capital punishment was any deterrent to crime. During my eight years as a State Representative, I do not recall that we ever passed her legislation, but we came closer each year. And throughout those years and for many years thereafter, no Governor ever signed a death warrant in the Commonwealth of Massachusetts.

No Governor ever again seemed sure enough of a verdict to play God with human life. No Governor ever wanted to be remembered as another Alvin T. Fuller, who signed the death warrants for Sacco and Vanzetti. All around them were living mortals who could remind them that if you electrocute an innocent man, you create a martyr whose ghost will haunt you through the ages.

I realize that as the century comes to an end crimes are more numerous and criminals are more vicious. And guilt can often be proven with scientific accuracy. But still a few state-mandated deaths do not reach the root-causes of the criminality of our culture.

Sacco and Vanzetti were right that if they had lived they would have had little influence upon society, despite their efforts to propagandize their point of view; but as martyrs, they will be remembered forever and they greatly advanced the cause of human rights.

The cause is kept alive in Boston today by an annual memorial service at the Community Church of Boston in Copley Square. The few remaining relatives and friends of Sacco and Vanzetti attend, and an award is made annually to someone who has struggled effectively for human rights. The small attendance is augmented each year by a few young people whose hearts are stirred by injustice and who share the dream of a less violent world.

When I entered the hall for the 1979 memorial service, I noticed a friend sitting alone just a few rows ahead of me – a man about 45, 5'8" tall, black hair. He had just been defeated in his campaign for re-election as Governor of Massachusetts. No bodyguards. No State Police. In fact, no hangers-on – because it was generally believed that his political career was over.

Paying tribute to the memory of Sacco and Vanzetti was the Honorable Michael S. Dukakis! Just two years earlier he had issued a Proclamation clearing their names!

Mike was the Democratic Party's candidate for President in 1988, yet eight years later it treats him as a pariah! He marches to a different drummer! So did Sacco and Vanzetti!

Chapter 14

INTERVIEW WITH JUSTICE BRANDEIS

"If we would guide by the light of reason, we must let our minds be bold."
Louis D. Brandeis

Clement A. Norton of Hyde Park, Massachusetts, (1894-1979) and Justice Louis D. Brandeis of the United States States Supreme Court (1856-1941) didn't seem to have very much in common.

Clem was a kind of street-fighter, who had lifted himself by the bootstrap of education to be the most effective politician in Boston during many pre-World War 2 years. Justice Brandeis was a learned legend in his own time. Yet, they respected and enjoyed each other.

When I first met Clem Norton in 1937, he was a phenomenon! He knew more about everything than anyone I had ever known. He loved people. He loved Boston. And he loved politics. All over the world, the shakers and the doers were his friends.

My first newspaper job after graduating from Dartmouth College with the Class of 1937 was as a reporter for the Hyde Park Gazette at $10. per week. And my first interviewee was Clem Norton, then the City Councillor from Ward 18 of Boston (Hyde Park). I called him:

"Mr. Norton. I am a new reporter for the Gazette. I admire what you have been doing in the city, and I would like to do a story on you.

"Sure," came Clem's voice booming over the telephone. "I have a meeting tonight in Forest Hills. I'll pick you up at 7 p.m."

That was the beginning of a lifelong friendship. I became a student of politics, and Clem was my mentor. He was a fast and fascinating talker. He was interested in everything, and he was a storehouse of information on everything.

What astonished me at first was that an Irish-Catholic politician – and a successful one – could be so anti-clerical:

"You have to realize that Boston is more Irish than Dublin and more Catholic than Rome," Clem would explain.

"We are a church-ridden people. We can't do anything unless we get the approval of men who go around in ladies' dresses.

"The church has developed an incredible system for separating people from their money. Do you know you can't even go to the bathroom in a Catholic Church?" That was news to me!

"They get you there only long enough to take the offering. Then they want you out. No toilets!"

No love was lost for Catholics in the Protestant circles in which I grew up – but this was the first time I had ever heard a Catholic speak critically of his own faith.

But Clem had his good reasons. Everything he stood for was opposed by his own church. He supported books (free of censorship!) and libraries and YMCAs and the separation of church and state. And he was the only Irish-Catholic politician in Massachusetts who was sincerely and energetically for Franklin D. Roosevelt and the New Deal.

The Fitzgeralds and the Kennedys and Jim Farley (FDR's Postmaster General) were doing their ducking and their dodging to advance their own political and economic interests. Clem really believed in the Roosevelt programs. He expounded them from his forum in the Boston City Council. The White House knew of his informed support and FDR appreciated it.

James M. Curley was Clem's nemesis during the heyday of

their careers. Curley came out on top – going on to Mayor and Governor and to the Federal penitentiary at Danbury, Connecticut! I was learning that often in politics the bad guy manages to beat the good guy!

Mayor Curley was king-pin in Boston through many of the years between the First and Second World Wars. Only Clem, from his seat on the Boston City Council, ever challenged him effectively.

But Boston was not Clem's only beat. He seemed to have friends all over the world. He gave me some of the best advice that I ever received:

"If you ever need information, ask for it. Any great leader who is really serving the public will be glad to answer your questions. Send a penny postcard." That is all they cost in those days, and Clem sent many.

Eamon deValera, the Prime Minister of Ireland. Clem talked about him as though he were a brother. I think now that they must have become close friends around 1919, when deValera came to America to persuade Woodrow Wilson to support the creation of an Irish republic. Write to Einstein – to Brandeis. Don't hesitate to ask.

Clem accumulated a whole room full of answers. When I first knew him in the late 1930s, he was Superintendent of Commonwealth Pier, a Civil Service post won by examination. His entire north wall of a very large office was covered with an array of four-drawer steel files.

I heard about nylon stockings and instant coffee from Clem, long before their inventions were common knowledge!

He may have received a law degree in the days when a Bachelor degree was not required. But he was largely self-educated – book-educated!

After World War 2 and after his retirement, he practically lived at the Boston Public Library. The staff kept a special cubicle for him, and in the 1950s, I often encountered him in Copley

Square, near the Library.

Clem was impressed when I became a featured columnist for The Boston Globe in 1942, and even more so when I was elected to the Massachusetts Legislature in 1948. He shared his remarkable friends with me:

"Would you like to meet Supreme Court Justice Brandeis?"

"Sure," I replied. "How do we arrange that?"

"We'll drive down to see him next Saturday at his Cape summer home." And we did.

Louis D. Brandeis was one of the all-time great Justices of the United States Supreme Court. He was famous for his lucid opinions and even more famous for his thundering dissents during the Hoover Administration and in the early Roosevelt years before FDR was able to make some changes.

"Holmes and Brandeis dissenting" was a war-cry that echoed throughout the country in the days of my youth. Holmes was Justice Oliver Wendell Holmes, Jr., (1841-1935) learned son of a famous Boston doctor. His father wrote the poem: "Old Ironsides."

Junior had volunteered for military service in the Civil War: "A man who would lead must share in the felt dangers of his times." Lawyers from different backgrounds – different cultures, different heritages, different religious faiths – but united in learning and in public service.

Their dissents fired the complaints against unemployment and poverty and defended trade unions. They alerted the country to the protections written into the Constitution and to the right of Congress to take reasonable steps to protect the "general welfare."

Justice Brandeis was born in Louisville, Kentucky, on November 13, 1856. He studied at Harvard Law School from 1875 to 1878, and is still revered for the best academic record ever achieved there.

He stayed in Boston and built a successful practice – serving some corporate interests on major questions, yet devoting much time to such pro bono projects as the creation of Massachusetts Savings Bank Life Insurance. People of modest means could buy life insurance at reasonable cost at their local bank.

He met and advised President Woodrow Wilson in 1912, and was nominated and confirmed as a Supreme Court Justice in 1916, after a bitter struggle. His opposition held two things against him: he would be the first Jew ever to serve in high Federal office, and he was a courageous and effective champion of the public's interests.

Some of the conservative Senators who fought confirmation were not charmed by the fact that in his youth Brandeis had written a book entitled: Other People's Money – and How the Bankers Use it.

I remember the Brandeis summer cottage, in Chatham I think, as a sunstruck white house overlooking a salt marsh and set well back from the highway. It was sparsely furnished. Mrs. Brandeis greeted us and led us to the Justice.

"Clem It's wonderful to see you again. I am delighted that you could drive down." He was genuinely glad to see the Boston City Councillor, and to get a first-hand report on Massachusetts politics. Clem introduced me and I listened with some awe.

The Justice was not without information on Boston and Massachusetts activities. Professor Felix Frankfurter of Harvard Law School had been sending his best students to the Supreme Court as law clerks, and one each year served Brandeis.

"How is Savings Bank Life Insurance doing?" he asked eagerly. "I always felt that if I could save a man a dollar, that was just as good as putting a dollar in his pay envelope."

He had invented the over-the-counter system before World War I as a workingman's answer to the rip-offs of the door-to-door collections required by the major companies. It had done well in Massachusetts, and had been copied in New York and in New Jersey. But then the great national companies slammed the door on any further expansion.

This conversation sparked my interest in the whole subject of life insurance coverage and reasonable premiums. I came to know Ed Goldberg , the conscientious state actuary, who produced rates substantially below anything else available in the United States.

And this led to one of my best "scoops" as a reporter for The Boston Globe after World War 2. I was sent to interview the new chief of the Veterans Administration, Carl Gray. I queried him about the National Service Life Insurance policies that had been provided for every G.I.

"When does the V.A. plan to pay a dividend on NSLI?" I asked. He had never heard the question raised.

"But, General," I protested. "Those rates that we are asked to pay are based upon old longevity tables – dating back to around 1918 I think. We are living about five years longer now. The V.A. should kick back some of our premium money, and even lower the premiums."

He was not happy to hear my questions or my information. Somewhat flustered, he ended the interview and promised to look into the matter. An exclusive story in The Boston Globe gave him a strong, public reminder of his promise!

About six months later, the V.A. announced that its experience with NSLI had been so favorable that it could now pay every insured GI a substantial dividend. It has been paying dividends ever since!

Our second visit with Justice Brandeis occurred at his apartment in Washington, D.C., after his retirement from the Court. I was struck by his gaunt appearance, his tall height and his shock of snow-white hair. This time the talk turned to Danish folk schools:

"Marvelous country, Denmark. They have a marvelous school system, and a great tradition of learning – everywhere and at all ages. Lighted school-houses for adult education." The Justice extolled the system at length and with great familiarity.

Sixty-five years have passed since Justice Brandeis spoke up for Danish folk schools, and suddenly his wisdom is more timely than ever. Welfare mothers are compelled to enter job-training. Welfare fathers are compelled to find work. The social burden that has been carried by the Federal government is being shifted back to unready states and local communities.

Who baby-sits with the children? Who cares for them after school? Who offers some recreational areas and some adult supervision? Why should costly school facilities be idle after 3 p.m. and throughout the week-ends? Concerned taxpayers had better take a look – at long last! – at Danish folk schools.

The rule used to be – anybody who wants to teach something can teach! Anyone who wants to learn something can learn! Those are still useful rules!

When Justice Brandeis first brought up the subject of the Danish folk schools, I did not understand why he thought it deserved top priority. I understood better after I visited Denmark – and saw some of the schools in action. . . Men as well as women care for children at the earliest ages. Social service workers visit and serve the needy in their homes. There are books everywhere, no visible policemen – schools are day-and-night community centers.

Denmark is one of the world's most civilized countries; Brandeis was one of our most civilized leaders. An affinity!

As we were about to leave the Washington apartment of the Justice, I asked him if I could take his picture. I had brought along my folding Kodak, and was praying that a tricky flash-unit would fire "in sync." That was a real problem in those days!

"I don't think so," the Justice replied slowly. "I have passed the age when one should have his picture taken." Then he changed his mind as we approached the door: either he wanted to do me a favor or he had a premonition that this time should be an exception to his rule.

I framed that gaunt head and shoulders and the shock of white hair in my view-finder and pressed the cable-release. The flash bulb fired and later development proved that the synchronization had worked. A miracle!

That was the last photo ever taken of Justice Louis D. Brandeis. It appeared on page one of The Boston Globe when he died just a few days later. Thirty years later Dean Erwin N. Griswold accepted the negative for the archives of Harvard Law School and fifty years later my original framed and enlarged print joined the extensive Brandeis collection at the School.

Brandeis and Holmes were two unsurpassed monuments to learning and integrity in the 20th century. Two amusing stories about them deserve to be remembered:

During the final years of their service together on the Supreme Court – in the 1930s – both of the Justices were in their 80s. But they often walked together near the Capitol en route to the Court. One day they passed two voluptuous young ladies walking along to their jobs on the Hill.

"Lovely young ladies," Brandeis is said to have commented.

"Ah," sighed Holmes, "to be fifty again!"

That story fits well with his known proclivities when he returned to his home city of Boston. He was a regular patron of the Old Howard, the largest and best burlesque theater in Boston. Even during the many years that he was a sitting Justice, he offered no apologies and never tried any disguise.

The best-known Justice in America could hardly hide his identity. He was too tall, too white-haired, too aristocratic and too well-dressed. And even if he could change all those well-known characteristics, no-one else ever had a handle-bar moustache as prominent as his.

Those were the days of Ann Corio and Gypsy Rose Lee and other beautiful maidens who did not hesitate to enchant the faithful regularly at the Old Howard. And Justice Holmes was among the most faithful. He would take his seat in about the third row of the right-front corner of the orchestra, – and on with the show!

It was almost like a command performance in London. Only when royalty is seated comfortably does the performance begin!

Justice Holmes was married to a notorious homebody whose claim to fame is that she once said:

"Washington is full of great men – and the women they married in their youth."

I wonder how she felt about her husband's frequent visits to the Old Howard?

Much of this I might have missed except for the continuing friendship of Clem Norton. My mentor also taught me that in public service it is often difficult to tell the good guys from the bad guys. And a bad guy on one issue may be your best ally on the next.

The muck-raking journalist, Lincoln Steffens, had discovered this truism decades earlier and he had chronicled his impressions in his Autobiography – seminal reading in my freshman year at Dartmouth College. He concluded in essence: "Beware of the Good Government guys; they may be stealing you blind."

As an on-going part of my political education, Clem set up a meeting with E.J. Brehaut, the executive director of the Boston Chamber of Commerce, at the North Shore home of Thomas Joyce – then and for many years later the most influential lobbyist in Massachusetts.

They shared with Clem at least three things in common: they loved politics; they liked to talk about it; and they knew just about everything that was going on.

Brehaut remained my good friend through the many years that he labored on behalf of Boston business interests. Agreeing with Tom was more difficult, because he was the king of the special interests.

Often, in later years, he represented what Clem called "the power trust." The private utility companies, then and now, were constantly under financial and political pressure. They controlled whole states and many prominent politicians – one way or another.

They managed to elect outright champions of their special interests, such as U.S. Senator Styles Bridges of New Hampshire. He spent most of his public career railing against the Tennessee Valley Authority and the Rural Electrification Administration – any effort to bring public power to poor people.

Private power interests also worked in subtle ways to reward their friends and punish their enemies. Their fine hand ran an annual "Clover Club" bash on St. Patrick's Day in Boston – seemingly just fun and games. But it was more than that!

The champion of public power throughout the New Deal years was the National Popular Government League – and that "League" was Judson King of Takoma Park, outside of Washington, D.C. He ran a kind of citizens' empire out of his home – and Clem and I did what we could to support him.

The peak of Clem Norton's fame came during the Presidency of John F. Kennedy. Clem had known him since he was a child, and when JFK ran for Congress in 1946, Norton referred to him as "the kid."

But during our early manhood and our first political years, both Jack Kennedy and I had known Clem well, and we had come to regard him with the same filial affection.

One day during his White House years, Jack heard that Clem was in Washington. He turned to faithful Dave Powers.

"Dave. Have someone go find Clem Norton. Arrange to pick him up for dinner at the boat tonight."

Clem was the guest of honor on the Presidential yacht, the Honey Fitz, named after the President's maternal grand-father – a former Mayor of Boston. The sultry evening breezes of the lower Potomac rang with rollicking stories of the old days in Boston.

That was as close as Clem ever came to national honor, but it was a nice gesture by a good President – and Clem deserved it!

He lived to an advanced old age. He out-lived most of the

people who had known him in his powerful days as a member of the Boston City Council and the Boston School Committee. He will be remembered mostly by younger generations as Charles F. Hennessey in Edwin O'Connor's Last Hurrah, a novel about Curley's Boston.

Author O'Connor caught the staccato speech and the exuberance of Clem in his Hennessey character:

"Oh, my dear man. Winning is not everything. No. No. . . The thing is to take the matter to the people; let them know what's going on, to fight the good fight and to tell the truth! Marvelous!

"I'll be in my sound truck on every corner in the city every night of the campaign, lashing away at them all! I'll stand on the sidelines and harass away, harass away! Marvelous!

"They fear it. They fear it more each year.

"One man telling the truth to the people! A time-bomb!"

With due respect to Edwin O'Connor, Clem was not as shallow or funny as he was made out to be in the Hennessey character. He was a kind of "time-bomb" in a city that needed one, and now and then he went off with reverberations that can still be heard.

Clement A. Norton of Hyde Park died on August 10, 1979.

His funeral was held in the Church of the Most Precious Blood, the Catholic church in his home ward. As I entered his church for the first time, I could not help wondering if there were any toilets available to the congregation!

I was one of only five persons present to honor him. Sic transit gloria!

(If my Boston Latin School lessons are still with me, that means – so passes glory.)

Chapter 15

THE GREAT AND GENERAL COURT

The Massachusetts Great and General Court may be the most ancient legislative body in the western world. At least, it had been in use for more than three hundred years when I was elected to the body in 1948. And I was the 59th member of my family to serve.

When word of my election hit the Boston newspapers, I began to receive some interesting phone calls. The first came from an excited young lady:

"Hi. Congratulations. I am your cousin."

My cousin? How could she be my cousin? I had eight cousins, and I had known them all since childhood. This sweet voice did not belong to any of those.

"My cousin?"

"Well. Your second cousin. Your mother and my mother were cousins, and dear friends. My favorite grandmother and your favorite grandfather were brothers and sisters."

"Where have you been all my life?"

"Well. I was born in Nanking."

Light dawned. Mother's favorite cousin had gone to China as a Congregational missionary shortly after World War 1. I remember her writing to her, and speaking fondly of "Flora." This young lady would be her child.

"You are?"

"Betty Lou Dieterich. Masters degree in social work from

the University of Chicago. New position in Boston."

Betty Lou was invited to the family Christmas party in Hyde Park. And I heard from her again after my first triumph in the House in the spring of 1949. I had discovered that blacks were still segregated in the Massachusetts National Guard even though the Army was abandoning the practice. A bill I had filed to end the segregation was dumped unceremoniously by the more aged members of the Committee on Military Affairs. But they had to send their adverse report to the House floor.

A handful of us who had served in World War 2 thought we could overturn the Committee report if we could force a roll-call. It took eighteen standing members to force a recorded vote. We found them; we persuaded them; they stood. We overturned the Committee by a roll-call vote of 147 for ending segregation – 45 for upholding the status quo. This was the beginning of a decade of civil rights history-making in Massachusetts.

Betty Lou was the first person to express her approval, and she did so in poetry:

"Oh there was a young fellow
"Who was anything but yellow
"Specially when he had to fight to win,
"And the noise that he raises
"It echoes like the blazes
"And that's why the votes roll in!
"Hiporay – hiporay
"That's why the votes roll in
"'Cause when Putnam gets to talking
"There's no more use in balking
"For victory is bound to come his way!"

After years of isolation in my all-male world of high school, college and the armed forces, I had never met a female so much on my wave length as Betty Lou. Must have been in our genes.

I spent eight years in the Massachusetts House, and I look

back upon them with many fond memories and with much satisfaction. Some politicians of my generation were great leaders –
John F. Kennedy and Edward W. Brooke, for example – but they
never seemed entirely comfortable in a legislative setting and they
never left any monumental legislative achievements. On the con-
trary, I loved the give-and-take of legislating and debating and
compromising and losing and winning. And I won often enough
to have something to cheer about now.

We banned the sale of fireworks to children. We won a bitter fight to fluoridate the public water supplies, probably the greatest public health advance of the 20th century. We authorized married women to teach in the public schools. We expanded the
University of Massachusetts, and created the state medical school
in Worcester.

We ended the perpetual campaigns for state offices by
extending the terms of Governor and lesser officials to four years.
We tried to end the Governor's Council, an anachronism that
remains from Colonial days, and tried to make minor statewide
officers appointive, but one cannot win them all.

We forbade the dumping of toxic wastes in state waters,
and off Cape Cod created the first state ocean sanctuary in
America. We expanded the state beach and park systems, and preserved hundreds of acres of land in Needham between Route 128
and the Charles River into the Leslie B. Cutler state park.

After ending discrimination in the Massachusetts National
Guard, we created a Fair Educational Practices Commission, and
then the Massachusetts Commission Against Discrimination –
models for other states and eventually the nation.

Our drumbeat of criticism of the land damages scandals in
the state highway program eventually forced the removal of a
Judge and an order from the Massachusetts Supreme Court for the
Attorney General to appear and to testify. I went to watch our aged
and august Court deal with the flamboyant Attorney General.
When the questions turned hot, he popped up out of the witness

chair and refused to testify further.

Chief Justice Stanley Qua – aged, gaunt, white-haired – leaned forward from the bench, and leveled his finger at the witness.

"Mr. Kelly. You will remain in your seat. And you will testify in this court – just like any other witness."

A succession of such performances doomed the Democratic ticket in 1952. Governor Paul A. Dever completed the doom scenario with his keynote performance at the Democratic National Convention during the summer. Under scorching television lights for the first time, the speakers had not learned to cope with profuse sweating.

Dever's demise was speeded by the earned nickname of "Porky Paul."

Three of my favorite legislative achievements are in the field of recreation. I had loved sports as a boy, and believed that every child deserved abundant opportunities.

When the Boston Bruins abandoned the Boston Arena in favor of the Boston Garden, I filed a bill for the state to acquire it for schoolboy hockey. I convinced Governor Christian A. Herter that it would be prudent for him and the party to do something helpful for inner city kids – and he agreed to sign the bill. It became a mecca for schoolboy hockey for something like forty years. It is now the home rink of Northeastern University.

During my college days, I was a speedskater, and I was painfully aware of the constant need for good ice surfaces. Then in 1949, I discovered that Toronto, Canada, had constructed open, artificial ice surfaces in its public parks. I filed a bill for Greater Boston parks to do the same. This was a new idea – never tried in the United States, perhaps never possible because of our slightly warmer climate.

But the idea caught on. Clifford Meadows, the Canadian engineer, came to Boston to explain the technical possibilities. And Senator John Powers, the chairman of the Joint Committee that would hear the bill, agreed to support it. I was home.

Massachusetts has now built about twenty-eight artificial ice rinks in Greater Boston parks. Olympic Champion Nancy Kerrigan learned her magic on the Stoneham rink. Robbie Ftorek of Needham became such a great skater that he packed the Boston Garden while only a captain of a high school hockey team. He went on into the National Hockey League, and for a time was the manager of Wayne Gretsky. Several Greater Boston boys have gone on now to the NHL.

The skating program never would have flown without the bi-partisan efforts of Senator Powers and Representative Putnam. I welcomed a chance to repay the Powers favor. He had long resented the fact that wealthy people along the Charles River Basin benefited from the constant water level of the river, made possible by a state dam, but that his poorer constituents in South Boston were not allowed to benefit in the same way.

He wanted Pleasure Bay, adjacent to the historic fort at Castle Island, enclosed by a dam – that would permit tidal cleansing but still maintain a constant water level for swimming. The Powers plan seemed reasonable to me, and a legitimate state expenditure – just as legitimate as the millions spent over two hundred plus years to improve the Charles River Basin.

If you fly into the Boston airport, you can look out your window on the left side of the plane, and see Pleasure Bay – just before your plane skims over Boston Harbor. In the warm summer months, you will observe thousands of people enjoying the park and the beach – the tidal flats gone forever!

Some narrow leaders of my party were apoplectic when I swung enough Republican votes to bring a victory to Senator Powers on this issue. Who laughs last? I do.

Those were good years in the Great and General Court of Massachusetts. I think those 58 Putnams who preceded me in this historic legislative body would agree that I kept the faith. I gave it my best shot.

A PROGRAM OF ACTION...

Rep. Putnam Skating Rink Bill Now Law

G.O.P. Education Program Drafted By Rep. Putnam

Rep. Putnam Raps Neglect of Education System in State

The Boston Herald says:

" ... outstanding ... has demonstrated considerable ability ... excellent speaker ... makes a striking appearance."

Putnam Condemns Plan to Create New State Agency

Commission Backs Putnam's Measure On Milk Grading

Rep Putnam Moves To Save Housing For Wartime Vets

Putnam Talks to High Schoolers on 'Loyalty Week'

Putnam Urges Simplified State Income Tax Forms

VFW Post to Show Putnam Films To Members

Dedham Out $6,720 Says Rep. Putnam

Rep. Putnam to Be Town Meeting Of Air Announcer

Needham Was Zealous for Welfare of Servicemen in Its Prompt Housing Construction

Rep. Putnam to Speak for the Milk Commission

Re-elect HAROLD PUTNAM
REPRESENTATIVE
DEDHAM... CANTON... NEEDHAM
REPUBLICAN PRIMARY   **SEPTEMBER 19, 1950**

HAROLD PUTNAM, 315 WARREN ST., NEEDHAM, MASS.

Chapter 16

BLACK AND WHITE

Prejudice against black people never seems to have existed in my family, which is very unusual in times that were rife with racial prejudice.

My father never had a good word for Jews or Catholics, but he thought the only black man in town was a nice fellow.

And when he observed my interest in civil rights, he once reported casually that his grandmother had taken him when he was a little boy to hear Booker T. Washington!

Booker T. Washington? Washington was the Reverend Martin Luther King, Jr., of his generation. He was the leader after the Civil War in demanding trade school educations for black boys. And he had come to Boston - and to my father's town of Milton - to raise money for his Tuskegee Institute in Alabama.

Recently I checked with the Milton, Massachusetts, Public Library: "Did Booker T. Washington ever speak in Milton in the early part of the 20th century?"

Yes! Back came a copy of an old clipping. Booker T. Washington spoke at the First Parish Church in Milton on December 12, 1904. My father would have been thirteen, attending the meeting with his grandmother, Lucinda Ross Barnes (1839-1921).

The abolition spirit of my Congregational forebears was alive and well in 1904, and I have nurtured it ever since.

I met only one black at my boys' camp (Charles E. Gary), one black at Boston Latin School (John "Moe" Robinson) and one black in my Dartmouth '37 class (George Arnold). That was the "token" representation in those days. All have been significant achievers, and all have been my lifelong friends.

But this inclination became serious in 1952, just after lawyer Edward W. Brooke and I - along with John F. Kennedy - had been named "Greater Boston Young Men of the Year."

I was a State Representative, laboring to complete my studies at Boston University Law School. And I was talking earnestly with Clarence Elam on a sidewalk at the back of the State House in Boston. Clarence and I were doing our best to elect Brooke to the House from a district in black Roxbury. But I was distracted by a beautiful girl crossing the street just behind Clarence. A beautiful black girl!

"Who's that?" I asked Clarence, motioning for him to look over his shoulder. "Oh. That's Glendora. . . Glendora McIlwain. . . She was in law school with Ed." (Boston University Law School, '48).

Glendora was special to me immediately for several reasons. I had never seen or heard of a black, woman lawyer. It was torturous enough to try to be a white, male lawyer - such was my thinking. The young lady was beautiful and graceful as she went trippingly on her way to a back door of the State House. She was dressed immaculately. She carried herself in a professional manner. She had received a degree that I had not yet earned! I made a mental note . . . Glendora McIlwain!

Fate was to join us three times in the next few weeks, first at the Republican State Convention where we were both Sergeants-at-Arms, and then at the Crispus Attucks Republican Club - named for the black sailor who was the first colonist to die in the revolution against England.

As head of the speakers bureau for the campaign, I had sent the three top state leaders to this inner-city opportunity - Christian A. Herter, Sumner G. Whittier and George Fingold - and I went myself to report on the substantial progress we had made in the State Legislature on civil rights.

We had a small audience that barely outnumbered the speakers , but conspicuously in the second row were - Edward W. Brooke, beginning the career that made him the only black male ever elected to the United States Senate by popular vote; attorney Glendora McIlwain, and her father, Simon P. McIlwain, one of the founders of the political club. We all met formally and exchanged pleasantries.

Scarcely a week later I thought it prudent to attend a dance in Westwood, Massachusetts, that honored Henry McLaren, the head of the State Veterans' Bonus division. If I were to progress up the ladder from the House to the State Senate and then to Congress, I would need solid support in Westwood.

When I walked into the hall a dance was in progress and the floor was thronged. But sitting alone on the sidelines was a pretty, black girl - Glendora McIlwain! - her blackness accentuated by a white dress.

Would it be "politic" in this lilly-white community for me to greet this stranger in a friendly way? Would all eyes follow me - a much-publicized State Representative - if I walked over and took a seat beside her?

My natural inclinations prevailed: "Miss McIlwain? Would you like to dance?"

Glendora was relieved and pleased to be accepted into the friendly throng. I thought it prudent to confess that I was not a great dancer, but that I wanted a chance to talk to her.

"You made it through B.U. Law School?"

"Yes - in 1948."

"Wow! That's a tremendous accomplishment. I am going through it now, and with everything going on at the State House, it seems impossible to get through all those exams. . . Where do you live?"

"Methuen."

"That's a long way from Westwod. How are you going to

get home?"

"I take a train from the North Station to Lawrence."

"How are you going to get to the North Station?"

"One of the girls from the office will give me a ride, but they may not want to leave in time for me to get the last train."

"I'll give you a ride. Can you meet me at the front door in fifteen minutes?"

"That would be fine. . . I would appreciate it."

The ride to Boston was an opportunity to learn more about her than her public "persona." She was born in Lugoff, South Carolina, on July 25, 1923. Her father was educated at a Methodist College, established by northern abolitionists after the Civil War, and he brought the family north to escape the violent racism of South Carolina. He studied at very opportunity and almost finished law school himself.

Glen had grown up in Lawrence and Methuen - Sunday school, public school and the Y.W.C.A. She was an exceptional student and an exceptional leader. Her father wanted her to obtain her undergraduate degree in a black girls' college, so he sent her back south to Bennett College in the Carolinas, from which she graduated in 1945.

I did not miss the personal details. She was single, did not seem to have a boyfriend, was twenty-seven years old and was dedicated to her profession and to a public service career. Male hunch - neglected in the loving department?

Both of us seemed to enjoy the ride, and the opportunity to get to know each other better. I did not want her to get away without exploring the possibility of seeing her again. As she stepped out of the car at the North Station, I summoned up my courage:

"Glen. I enjoyed being with you. . . Couldn't we have lunch some day?"

"Sure. . . I would like that."

"How do we arrange it?"

"Just call me at the Bonus Office. I can meet you at the corner of Bowdoin Street and Ashburton Place at the back of the State House."

"How about noon tomorrow?"

"Fine. . . I'll be there. . . Night. . . And thanks for the ride."

For three years Glen and I had lunch regularly once a week. And we must have set a world's record for a platonic relationship between two people in the prime of life, but it served our purposes at that time. Glen dreaded having to tell her parents that she was in love with a white male, and I dreaded the end of my political progress and any disruption of my family obligations.

I found her an enchanting female, and as I tumbled out bold ideas I intended to pursue in the Legislature, she might whisper softly: "Pirate." I did not understand at first, because I have great respect for the law and am non-violent in my views. She meant it as a compliment - that I was fearless. Black males cannot risk being fearless - it often costs them their lives. Fearlessness was a precious new feeling for Glendora.

The relationship became more serious about the time that my career took me to Washington, D.C. Senator Leverett Saltonstall offered me the position of Counsel to the U.S. Senate Small Business Committee, and with three children heading for college I could not afford to miss the opportunity. The details were worked out by his Administrative Assistant, Charles W. Colson - ten years later the hatchet man for the scoundrels in the Nixon White House.

But gone were the weekly visits with Glendora. The next best was spending a week-end with her every two weeks - along with Saturday and Sunday visits to old clients and some P.R. work for our now big-time candidate, Edward W. Brooke. At 4 p.m. on Saturday afternoons, Brooke would ask with great curiosity - "same girl?" And for many years I would reply: "Same girl." He could not understand such total satisfaction with one girl!

My drive from the National Capitol to Boston every two weeks became so punctual and regular that the word went around the Hill that this was the best transportation to Boston. We could leave the Capitol garage at 4 p.m. on a Friday and be in downtown Boston at midnight. I began to attract a clientele.

Francis W. Sargent, later a Massachusetts Governor, rode with me at least once when he was a park planning consultant for Laurence Rockefeller. And an executive of the Library of Congress hitched a ride, and asked if he could bring along his young associate. Both were total strangers.

He fell sleep in the front seat at about the half-way point, and the young lady sitting behind me came to life - sitting forward on the back seat and chatting close to my head. Suddenly, I felt a warm hand creeping along my left thigh, between the driver seat and the door - apparently seeking a warm hand in return.

Aren't young ladies wonderful? And unpredictable?

My worst drives to Boston involve the record blizzards of the winter. Nothing could deter me from the urge to see Glendora, but the weather almost won two severe battles.

Once, my passenger was Donald Whitehead, a Nixon appointee to be Chairman of the Appalachian Regional Commission, but a native of Stoughton and with a home near Route 1. We were engulfed in snow shortly after leaving Washington, and it piled higher as we neared New York City and plowed ahead into Connecticut and Massachusetts. We could continue only by following plows as they fought to keep open the main roads.

I left Don in the middle of Route 1 in Stoughton about midnight - in doubt that I could ever reach Boston where Glen was waiting, anxiously I was sure. Two hours late. Crawling at about ten miles per hour, and at least twenty miles more to go. When I finally reached Boston, only Boylston Street was open to the heart of the city. Snow was piled six feet high along the street, and I could find no way to get off the road. My customary drug-store was closed and my usual public phone unavailable. How could I locate Glendora without alerting others to my search?

I had to walk to the hotel desk, ask for her by name and take the elevator up in clear view of the clerk. I feared the tabloid headlines: YANKEE POL IN TRYST WITH BLACK LADY. It never happened, and probably most people were not interested.

The other time we were to meet at the Lawrence train station, Glen driving her own car about ten miles. But again it was the worst blizzard of the winter, and I was lucky to get to Lawrence and a public phone.

"May I speak to Glendora, please."

"Just a minute." Mr. McIlwain always answered the phone, and he never asked: "Who's calling?" Instinctively, black people cover up other people's liaisons - in the slave days a busybody master would disrupt them. Her father never asked Glen who was calling.

Years later, I reflected that he must have known. There was no disguising my voice - he would have concluded that I was white, highly educated and very interested in his daughter. And knowing my legislative record for civil rights, even at that early stage, he might not have been against the relationship. Glen was fearful needlessly!

"Glen. I am in Lawrence and I think I can get to the bottom of Brookdale Avenue in fifteen minutes. Do you think you can get out?"

"I think so. . . Just wait there for me."

She had to walk a quarter of a mile, down a steep hill, through snow more than a foot deep - with the wind blowing blinding snow against her. No other cars were on the highway - so I waited at the appointed place.

Then watched a small speck in the distance emerge into someone bundled in a fur coat, head covered with a hood, boots reaching to the knees. Step by high step the speck came into focus as a frozen and breathless Glendora. She tumbled into the warmth of the car - and the warmth of my heart!

And in the middle of a blizzard and with the roads nearly

impassable, her parents had not asked her where she was going. Or whom she was going to meet!

But when she had recovered from the trek through the snow, she seemed sleepy.

"How come you seem so tired?"

"I didn't sleep very well last night. . . Some fresh kids were racing snowmobiles through our front yard,"

Without thinking, I asked a macho white man's question: "Why didn't your father tell the little bastards to get out?"

Glen seemed to gasp at the suggestion, and then said softly: "That would not have been a very prudent idea." Black men have lost their lives for lesser reasons! Black men fear to order white people – even white children – even to defend their own property.

Fortunately, we were not limited to snowy week-ends. Occasionally, she was able to visit Washington, D.C., particularly for civil rights matters while she was serving as an Assistant Attorney General at the State House in Boston. We were able to sit together in the gallery of the House of Representatives when Congress debated the Civil Rights Act of 1964.

We held our breaths when Congressman Howard Smith of Virginia, the southern cracker chairman of the Rules Committee, rose to offer an amendment - to insert the words "or gender" after the words "no discrimination on account of race or national origin."

"The S.O.B. has shot himself in the foot," I commented. "The House may go for it, and still approve the bill." Smith had hoped that his amendment would prevail, and that the woman-haters would join the black-haters and they could defeat the legislation. Didn't work out that way! The landmark legislation became law.

She also came to Washington for Dr. Martin Luther King, Jr.'s "March on Washington ." We had met him at the Boston Garden, when he considered a rally there, and we had supported him when the NAACP divided over his opposition to the Vietnam

War. We marched together for him in 1964, hand-in-hand from the Union Station to the Lincoln Memorial. We stood only fifty feet in front of him when he delivered his "I Have A Dream" speech.

We sensed that his life was about to be ended. We realized that history was being made. We knew that the legislative civil rights struggle was being won. And we were enthralled by the most powerful oration of the twentieth century.

But by 1964 our partings had become more agonizing. As two busy professional people, with important careers ahead of us, we had been able to return stoically to our duties for many years. But not any longer – there were tears in the eyes of the lady lawyer when the time came to say good-bye. And with the college educations of three children completed and with my chance of going to Congress ended with the defeat of Speaker Martin, the time had come to make a marital change.

The difficulties mounted. One week-end when Glendora spent Saturday night with me in Needham we were awakened on a Sunday morning by an insistent ringing of the front door-bell. Glen sat up in bed in terror – black people have good reason to fear unexpected calls at their front doors. I had an uneasy premonition that it was a tabloid reporter. It was! Two of them from the Boston American.

Many years earlier The Boston Globe had sent me on a similar assignment, and I had bumped into Richard Tregaskis, who was covering the same story for the Boston American – the Hearst paper. His personal questions so embarassed me that I felt great sympathy for the victim, and I did my best to end the inquisition. Tregaskis later wrote the World War 2 best-seller *Guadalcanal Diary.*

"We are looking for Glendora McIlwain." They made their mission clear. En garde!

I blocked the front door, making it perfectly clear that they were not going any further. "She doesn't live here."

"Where does she live?"

"With her parents on Brookdale avenue in Methuen." They

gave up easily, and left. We called Methuen to warn Glen's parents, who by that time knew everything.

I returned to my agitated lover, but next Sunday we could read the results of their quest in the roaring headlines on page one: "Yankee Pol to Wed Black Girl." For the first time ever, in my Boston Globe and Boston Herald town of Needham, the Sunday Boston Americans were piled four feet high in front of every local church. And they were hawked loudly by aggressive newsboys.

Things did not get any easier. In 1966, the Commonwealth of Massachusetts had a kicker in the divorce laws that prohibited the "guilty party" from remarrying within the state for at least two years. And the man was always considered the guilty party. We planned to marry just over the state line in New Hampshire, and insulated a cottage on Canobie Lake in which we could spend an idyllic winter. A little awkward for dedicated officials of Massachusetts.

The next year, without our knowledge or participation, the Great and General Court of Massachusetts (our legislature!) repealed the two-year ban. The legislators had concluded that a society that favors the institution of marriage should not be in the business of prohibiting it. I call it "the Putnam repealer." My thanks to the wise legislators of the Commonwealth!

Governor Frank W. Sargent appointed Glendora the Chairman of the Massachusetts Commission Against Discrimination, a position for which she had prepared all of her life and which she had helped to create. In 1970 I received a Presidential appointment as Regional Director of the United States Department of Health, Education and Welfare – to be based in the Kennedy Federal Building in Boston. And then a few years later, President Gerald Ford named Glendora Putnam to be Deputy Assistant Secretary of the United States Department of Housing and Urban Development, with an office in Washington.

Throughout those years she accepted increasingly important duties with the Y.W.C.A., which had helped to nurture her from girlhood in Lawrence. She became the President of the Boston Y.W.C.A., and then the National President in 1985. All of this made marriage not quite the total bliss that we had expected, and I sought a divorce in 1976.

She has become a trustee of her Alma Mater, Bennett College, and has received an honorary degree from Bennett and from Southeastern Massachusetts University. I honor her too –

I am privileged to have known and loved a great lady.

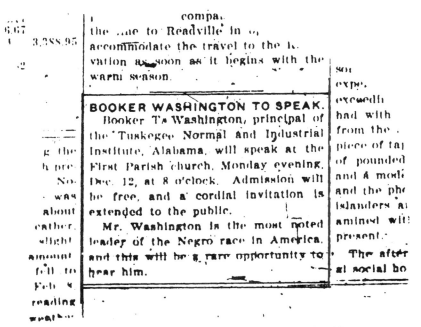

BOOKER WASHINGTON TO SPEAK.
Booker T. Washington, principal of the Tuskegee Normal and Industrial Institute, Alabama, will speak at the First Parish church, Monday evening, Dec. 12, at 8 o'clock. Admission will be free, and a cordial invitation is extended to the public.

Mr. Washington is the most noted leader of the Negro race in America, and this will be a rare opportunity to hear him.

Milton, Massachusetts, *Record,* December 10, 1904

Thanks to the Milton Public Library we know that Booker T. Washington *did* speak in Milton almost one hundred years ago.

Chapter 17

SPEAKER JOHN McCORMACK (1891-1980)

John W. McCormack of South Boston went to Congress from my district when I was only 12 years old (in 1928), and he stayed there until 1971 when I was 55.

For 42 years he was my Congressman, and for three-quarters of those years, he was also my friend. And he was a powerful friend – Majority Floor Leader from 1940 to 1961 (except for two GOP terms in 1947-1949 and 1953-1955) and Speaker of the House from 1962 to 1971.

John McCormack was a New Deal stalwart during the most exciting and productive decade of legislation in American politics – 1932 to 1942. The Social Security Administration, the Securities and Exchange Commission, the Works Progress Administration, the Civilian Conservation Corps, the Tennessee Valley Authority, the National Youth Administration, and later the G.I. Bill of Rights. He was the point man for the New Deal throughout the FDR years – with the President on everything except an occasional difference if the Pope took a different position, as he did on Franco Spain.

He was an experienced leader, a strong speaker, a special friend of the Jewish people who supported his stands and a conspicuously dutiful husband. He claimed to have had dinner with his wife every evening of their married life – an almost impossible task for anyone in public service! And he liked cigars!

He came to know me through my political column in the

Hyde Park Tribune from1938 to 1941, and then from my Victory Forum column in The Boston Globe until I entered the Navy in 1943. He was more than an attentive Congressman. He seemed to take a fatherly interest in my welfare and my progress. Perhaps not having any children of his own, he felt a paternal concern for me.

Busy as he must have been in Washington during his climb to leadership of the Democratic Party and the country, he wrote frequently – always on a typewriter and always ending: "Typed by me personally. John." I could tell – he made more typographical errors than I was accustomed to at the Globe.

I was especially appreciative of his correspondence during the years that I was at sea – 1943 to 1946 – or languishing in strange ports all over the world. He seemed to welcome my personal observations of foreign countries, and I welcomed his keeping me in touch with American politics. I never asked him for a favor and never had any occasion to need one – until the Christmas season of 1945.

I was the Armed Guard Officer in charge of a Navy gun crew on a merchant ship carrying ammunition for the invasion of Japan. We had crossed two oceans to reach the Pacific war zone. The atomic bomb had brought a cataclysmic end to the Pacific war, and our armada of ships at Okinawa was turned back as unneeded. We landed only briefly at Wakayama, and had seen the devastation that fire bombs alone had wrought. No living thing; no standing building. No grass. No trees.

"Proceed for home," came a terse Navy order. Hundreds of fully-laden Liberty ships began again the long haul across the Pacific. And in mid-ocean came a further order: "Destroy all Navy ammunition. Practice fire or throw overboard."

For us it meant cases of 20 m.m. machine-gun ammo, sleek 3″ shells and heavy 5″ shells – war heads backed by gleaming brass powder cases. Disposal crews worked for hours – some for days – consigning millions of dollars worth of ammunition to the Pacific deep.

When we headed up the East Coast , our ammunition was long gone. Our ammo lockers were empty and re-painted. Our quarters were cleaned for shore inspection. After six months at sea – rarely if ever getting a few hours on shore – we were super ready "to hit the beach."

And we reached the mouth of the Delaware River two days before Christmas! A local pilot came aboard with written orders: "Armed Guard Officer. Disembarking of Naval personnel delayed until after the holidays. All shore personnel on leave."

On leave! Couldn't send a liberty launch for men who had been at sea for six months? Couldn't do some paper work to free us from our floating prison? I seethed with anger at the injustice of it.

I had a healthy respect for Naval Regulations and a natural disdain for anyone who used "political influence," but the time seemed right to complain in the old American way: "Write your Congressman!" I had good reason to believe that Congressman McCormack would share my concern:

"Dear John," I wrote – "I hope this reaches you before you depart for Boston and Christmas. I and my Navy gun crew are imprisoned on a Liberty ship at the mouth of the Delaware River. We have been at sea for six months. Navy shore personnel intend to leave us here until after the holidays. We would be grateful for your efforts to secure disembarkation at once."

The Delaware pilot inched our ship slowly up the river, seeking an anchorage in the gray stillness of a dismal winter day. When he went over the side to his pick-up boat, I slipped my Special Delivery letter to him – addressed to Hon. John W. McCormack, Majority Floor Leader, Congress of the United States, Washington, D.C.

Twenty-four hours passed. Did the pilot mail the letter? Was the mail moving in the last hours of the day before Christmas? Then the radio crackled on Christmas Eve!

"Prepare to disembark all Naval personnel at 1100

Christmas Day." Signed: Port Director.

Nothing was ever said about what caused the change of heart along the Delaware shore on that cold and wintry day in the Christmas season of 1945.

Thanks, Mr. Speaker!

Yankee Journal

JOHN W. McCORMACK
12TH DIST. MASSACHUSETTS

EUGENE T. KINNALY
SECRETARY

Office of the Majority Leader
House of Representatives U. S.
Washington, D. C.

August 15,1944.

Ensign Harold Putna, USNR.,
S.S.West Keene,
℅ Fleet Post Office,
New YorkCity--NY.

Dear Harold;-

      I am in receipt of your last letter, and Iamglad
to hear from you.   I am glad that you like the Platform.
it is pleasing to me to note from your letter that you heard me
reporting the same to the Convention while you were at sea.
It has been favorably commented upon generally throughout
the country, particularly the peace plank.   Letushope that
after this war is over, something willbe done that will enable
the nextgeneration, the children of those serving in this war,
to live a normal, happy, peaceful life, and not to befaced with
the fear and spectre of war.   Unless something is done,
Harold, there willbe another one 25 or 30 years from now.
After two experiences inWorld Wars we oughtto have enough
reason existiting here and abroad to do those things that will
outlaw war for at least one generation, and if we do that, we
will leave something for the next generation to preserve and
improve upon.

      With kind personal regards, I am
P.S.Personally typed.   Sincerely,
    John.

JOHN W. McCORMACK
12TH DIST, MASSACHUSETTS

OFFICE OF THE MAJORITY LEADER
HOUSE OF REPRESENTATIVES
WASHINGTON, D. C.

I have read with deep interest Harold Putnam's reports on some of the countries he has visited. They have not only been educational to me, but informative and impressive as well. I was so impressed with his report on French North Africa that I sent a copy along to the State Department.

An intelligent foreign policy can only be based on widespread understanding of foreign countries and their peoples, and the conditions existing in those countries. Harold Putnam's lectures and pictures will be a big help, and in my opinion, of invaluable assistance, in spreading widely that much-needed understanding.

1946 - Endorsement of post-war travel lectures.

Chapter 18

SPEAKER THOMAS P. ONEILL, Jr. (1913-1994)

"Tip" O'Neill, one of the ablest Speakers of the Congress in this century, died in 1994 at the age of 81.

My clearest recollection of him goes back to the years when he was tall, dark and handsome – a young giant with coal black hair. That was in 1948, when he was the Speaker of the Massachusetts House of Representatives and I was a brand new member.

I had been elected by the Republican voters of Dedham, Canton and Needham – comfortable suburbs of Boston – and "Tip" was the leader of Democratic voters of the city of Cambridge. He was probably not completely happy with my election.

He knew me as the veterans' columnist for The Boston Globe, with a considerable following. And he knew that in 1940, I had managed a statewide campaign of Independents for Roosevelt and Wallace – so I was identifiable as a kind of non-partisan Republican. Those were somewhat rare in those days, as they are today.

After World War 2 in Massachusetts, the Democratic party was powerful, lazy and corrupt – at least that is the way it appeared to young men just out of wartime service. And the Republican party was not much better – totally dominated by rich, old Yankees, who were against extending any governmental benefits beyond their own privileged class.

"Tip" had always found it easy to defeat his opposition, when it stuck to its old leaders and its old ways – but he found it awkward to deal with young whipper-snappers like me who believed in equal rights for everyone and genuinely liked people of all religions, races and nationalities. During those early years in the Massachusetts House, O'Neill and Putnam – from very different backgrounds and with very different loyalties – labored under grudging admiration for each other.

After my successful election in 1948, the Speaker summoned me to his office to discuss committee assignments. I could choose two committees.

"Better give me your first choice and then your second choice," Tip advised.

"Some of the committees are more popular than others, but I'll do my best to place you where you really want to serve."

"Well, I'd like Education and Public Health," I told him.

Tip indicated that he could take care of those requests. They were not the most popular committees in the House – most of the Representatives sought assignments where they would have more control over state funds.

But I attributed whatever progress I had made in life to a good education-at Boston Latin School and at Dartmouth College – and I was anxious to see that the next generation of young people received equally good opportunities. I welcomed the chance to serve on the Education Committee – even though it was headed by big-city Democrats with whom I often disagreed.

First off we were hit with a hot issue – should married women be allowed to teach in the public schools?

"You mean they can't teach now, if they are married?" That's right, the older members of the Committee assured me. The Catholic Church opposed encouraging women to work outside the home, so that was the position of Democrat members, who were mostly of that faith.

Suppose they have been abandoned, but not divorced?

Suppose they are unable to have children? The majority was not interested in considering any exceptions.

Some of us who were younger and freer spirits managed to force the issue to a roll call vote on the floor of the House, and eventually the discrimination against married women was ended.

The Education Committee tackled some other interesting issues. We championed the expansion of the University of Massachusetts at Amherst, which was little more than an "aggie" school in 1949. And year after year, we insisted that the state should create a medical school. It finally came with the creation of a first-class medical complex in Worcester, the central city of our state.

I chuckle now when I note that Bill Cosby went to the University of Massachusetts for his doctorate in education, when famous athletes are treated by doctors at the Massachusetts Medical School in Worcester, and when scholarly articles and books are produced by a first-class faculty.

But all was not smooth progress during those four years from 1948 to 1952, when Tip and I were in the Massachusetts House together. He remained a powerful Speaker, and he ruled with an iron hand. But he was saddled with a Democratic administration deeply involved in corruption in the booming abundance of a highway program.

After ten years on the staff of The Boston Globe, it was easy for me to smell a story when I·encountered one. And to build it into headlines when all the elements were present. When I had the evidence in hand, I spilled the juicy details on the floor of the House. Eager reporters then and now like a controversy, and the press gallery would fill when I rose to add another chapter to an ongoing saga.

Some of my colleagues resented the publicity that was coming my way, but the Greater Boston Junior Chamber of Commerce named me a "Young Man of the Year" in 1951 – along with John F. Kennedy, later President, and Edward W. Brooke, later

United States Senator.

George Fingold led those who cheered me on. Christian A. Herter, Jr., later a top State Department official, and Christopher Phillips, later an important leader at the United Nations, would vote with me, but they never volunteered to lead the charge.

"I ought to have more help in the House," I complained to Fingold, then a Special Prosecutor on his way to being Attorney General. "Why don't young Herter and Chris Phillips get into the fight?" Both grew up in wealthy families with deep roots in public service and the Republican Party. And both were ambitious to carry on the family traditions.

George, who grew up in the slum that used to surround the Boston Garden, had a ready answer: "They never were in a good fight in their lives!"

But Tip had been in many a fight, and he was prepared in 1950 and 1951 to silence me – he wanted to see discussions of highway scandals off the House agenda. And he smashed two gavels in an effort to still the debate. He also had acquired a sneaky habit of turning down the volume on the floor microphone, if he did not like what he was hearing.

It was no easy task to smash a House gavel. I had never seen it happen before and I have never seen it since – either in Boston or Washington. The head was as big as a quart bottle, and the handle was at least a foot and a half long. Tip wielded it on a podium about ten feet higher than the floor microphone, and when he swung the gavel onto its massive base, the sound reverberated throughout the State House. There was no ignoring the command!

The first broken gavel resulted when I moved that the Democrat Attorney general be summoned to the House Chamber to explain what was going on in the land damages program in his office. By reading the fine print of the ancient rules, I had discovered authority for the summons, and noted that it had not been used in more than one hundred years.

"The gentleman from Needham is out of order," Tip shouted. "He will take his seat." All accompanied by the smashing of the gavel – and the head flying out onto the floor, nearly decapitating his Majority Leader.

I remained standing. "Point of order," I defended.

"The gentleman will state his point of order," anger noticeably mounting in the Speaker.

"If the Speaker will refer to the rules of the House and the ancient precedents for this motion, he will find that it is in good order and should be presented to this body." Tip hastily consulted Larry Groves, the saintly parliamentarian of the House, who always called them as he saw them from a lifetime of expertise and experience. I knew that Larry would recommend a ruling in my favor!

"The gentleman may proceed," the Speaker decided reluctantly. The motion failed to carry, but the point had been made and the furor over the highway scandals mounted. A judge was on the way to removal from the bench and the troubles of the Attorney General increased daily.

The second smashed gavel came when I moved that the legal questions involved in the highway corruption be transferred directly to the Supreme Judicial Court of Massachusetts.

Somehow I prevailed on that matter, and a few weeks later I watched Attorney General Francis E. Kelly squirm in the witness chair. I was still in law school. I felt a satisfying pleasure in seeing the law at work.

I didn't learn until later that Tip had a special reason for his anger in the House debate. His brother was an Assistant Attorney General! He was not involved in the highway mess, but his political fate and job security were wrapped up in the fate of the Attorney General – and Tip could foresee that Kelly would be defeated easily in 1952. That is what happened.

Tip went to Congress in 1952, taking the seat vacated by John F. Kennedy when he advanced to the Senate in the race against Henry Cabot Lodge, Jr. That spared him the anguish of being present during the revolution in party politics in the House. Irish/Catholic/Democrat control was ended – both the Republican and Democratic parties in Massachusetts were changed forever and for the better.

With Tip gone to Washington, we offered a Jew for Attorney General (George Fingold). We nominated a black lawyer (Edward W. Brooke) for Secretary of State. And we advanced an Italian Catholic into important positions in public service (John A. Volpe, later Governor). And I polled Republican members of the House to prove that two-thirds of our members were of non-Yankee origin.

We led repeated battles for civil rights legislation – no discrimination in education, no discrimination in public housing, no discrimination in the National Guard and a Massachusetts Commission Against Discrimination to enforce the new laws.

I think now that Tip learned from the changes that took place in Massachusetts. In Washington, as an increasingly powerful member of Congress, he became a leader for the national civil rights reforms that he had already observed taking place in his home state.

We accomplished the changes in the 1950s. Under the whip of the Rev. Martin Luther King, Jr. and then President Lyndon Johnson, the nation went along with the new civil rights in the 1960s.

Tip's political instincts were better than those of anyone else that I ever knew. His instant evaluations of character, loyalty and "guts" were uncanny. I don't remember him ever being wrong.

He did not like Sumner G. Whittier of Everett, with whom he served in the House after World War 2 and who almost became Governor in the 1950s. Whittier and I came from the same old Yankee backgrounds, and we shared many political ideals. So Tip used to kid me about Sumner!

"How's Sumner doing?" he would ask me. "Still ducking the big ones?"

Tip's theory was that no-one could count on Sumner when the pressure was on. He would illustrate his theory with his bag-of-groceries story.

The House was in a turmoil over a Republican effort to impose a state sales tax. The Democrats believed that this was an effort of rich Republicans to make the middle class and the poor pay for their own social services. They opposed the sales tax – and at one point Sumner agreed with them.

Tip claimed that Whittier brought a big bag of groceries to the floor of the House, and dramatically showed item by item what a sales tax would add to the cost of the basic necessities of life. Sumner was a forceful public speaker and he could be very dramatic.

"But where was Whittier when the vote came?" Tip would ask. "He voted in favor of the sales tax."

Friends of Sumner were painfully reminded of Tip's evaluation when Whittier was the odds-on favorite for the Republican nomination for Governor at the convention in Worcester in 1952. The hall reverberated with insistent chants of "We want Whittier."

Whittier was a kind of "people's choice." He made it plain that he was for the middle class and the poor, and even billed himself as a "three-decker" candidate. He and his wife, Jessie, and their three children lived in and owned a "three-decker" house in Everett – occupying one flat and renting out the other two.

All of this did not sit very well with the wealthy old Yankees who usually controlled the Republican party. They could tolerate a little of this independence at the House and Senate levels – but they rebelled at such a candidate advancing to Governor, however strong the yells in the convention hall and however certain would be Whittier's election in the campaign for Governor.

They swung their support to Christian A. Herter, then an experienced member of Congress – much less known throughout

Massachusetts than Sumner G. Whittier. As the convention balloting approached, Sumner was called backstage to meet with party leaders who controlled the purse-strings. We never learned exactly who was there or exactly what was said – but we had no doubts. We could guess accurately.

The major contributors to the party were there, and Sumner was told that if he proceeded in the balloting for Governor there would be no money for a successful campaign. If he withdrew, and allowed the Governor nomination to go to Herter, he would have full party support for Lieutenant Governor. Sumner caved in – as Tip would have predicted!

He could have had the nomination for Governor. He didn't need the big contributors. It was going to be a Republican year anyway – after all the Democratic corruption scandals we had unveiled in the House.

The basic difference between Sumner and Tip? Tip would have told those backstage warriors where they could stick their money. And he would have gone on to be Governor.

Tip went to Washington in 1953 as a new member of Congress, and I went there in 1959 as Minority Counsel to the United States Small Business Committee, working with and for Massachusetts Senator Leverett Saltonstall. My path did not cross Tip's very much until I went over to the House side around 1963 as Administrative Assistant to former Speaker Joseph W. Martin, Jr. – with an office that looked out upon the base of the dome of the Capitol.

Mr. Martin had been Speaker in the 1950s and Tip was on his way to being Speaker in the 1980s. They were friends – which seems strange today when one views the bitterness and hatred that prevails in Washington between party leaders. When James Milne retired as Mr. Martin's Administrative Assistant after about forty years with him, Tip was there for the ceremony when I took his place.

From 1948 to 1994, I followed the career of Thomas P. "Tip"

O'Neill, Jr., and my admiration for him grew with each passing year. He is remembered now for his doctrine that "all politics is local." But he will be remembered also for other principles – a good leader deserves loyalty and progress takes courage.

And he will be remembered for being the first major elected public official to openly oppose the Vietnam War. When Tip issued his statement, I was only a little surprised. It was more adventuresome than he usually was – but I knew that his children and their friends were educating him about what was really going on in Vietnam.

In my opinion, Tip's statement on the Vietnam War was the beginning of his move up the ladder from Cambridge "pol" to statesman. Ever after Tip was a voice to be reckoned with. And he was a voice to be heard.

Even in retirement, Tip never lost his fighting spirit. He never favored the adventures of the Reagan Administration in El Salvador and in Nicaragua – with death squads in the streets and even the murder of nuns. The Boland Amendment forbade such goings-on, but the White House paid no attention to the legal barrier – and it worsened the situation by switching Iran profits to Central American support.

Tip listened to reports from the Maryknoll Sisters, who were struggling to do Christ-like deeds in impoverished lands. He found the Maryknoll information more accurate and more reliable than what was coming from the Reagan C.I.A.

Finally, when Congress began digging into the illegal and ineffective mess, President Reagan blamed Tip "for stalling aid to the freedom fighters."

From a Cape Cod beach, Tip shot back: "Freedom fighters? I never regarded them as anything but rogues, bandits and thieves."

After his death, publications that did not have many kind words for him during his lifetime made some amends in thoughtful eulogies. The Wall Street Journal carried an interesting column by Albert R. Hunt, comparing the O'Neill career with that of Richard M. Nixon.

Hunt knocked Nixon for "deep character shortcomings and insecurities" despite a "towering intellect."

As to Tip, he wrote: "O'Neill was not a towering intellect, but his leadership was greatly enhanced by his personal character and his sure sense of himself."

Amen!

Yankee Journal

THOMAS P. O'NEILL, JR.
MASSACHUSETTS
MAJORITY LEADER

Congress of the United States
House of Representatives
Office of the Majority Leader
Washington, D.C. 20515

15 September 1975

Mr. Harold Putnam
2 Center Plaza
Room 220
Boston, Massachusetts

Dear Harold:

Many thanks for your recent letter enclosing photos of
your paintings.

They are beautiful, Harold, and I must say you bring
out the best in that lovely Irish countryside. Can you tell
me where Kilshanny is? I have mentioned this as the possible
home of my ancestors to many people who know Ireland, but
none of them can recall ever hearing of it.

Since my office is now being redecorated with paintings
of historical interest for the Bicentennial, I'll take a
raincheck on using the Kinvara painting to display. Meantime, if you have done anything along the lines of old
Boston, etc. I would be very honored to have it to use here.

With warm personal regards, and every good wish for a
most successful exhibit,

Sincerely,

Thomas P. O'Neill, Jr.

P.S. I have taken the liberty of keeping the photos - if
you'd like them returned let me know.

**1975 - Just back from an ecstatic trip to Ireland, the author gets the next
Speaker interested in his Irish ancestry!**

Chapter 19

GEORGE FINGOLD (1908-1958)

You can't keep a good man down. And during the 1950s, George Fingold was a good man for the Republican Party in Massachusetts.

In 1952, he became the first Jew ever elected to a statewide office in the Bay State, and in 1958, except for his untimely death, he would have been the first Jewish Governor.

For a boy born in the North End slum of Boston, near the site of the Fleet Center that now replaces the Boston Garden, George Fingold went far and did well.

We first began hearing about Fingold around 1950, when he was named Special Prosecutor to end corruption in the city of Fall River. His repeated headlines earned him the GOP nomination for Attorney General in 1952 – and for the first time ever a Massachusetts political party positioned a Protestant, a Catholic and a Jew on the same ticket. A concerted effort by young Republicans, just back from World War 2, produced a "balanced ticket," and it won easily.

During fierce debates in the House over corruption in the state highway program, I frequently went to Fingold for counsel and support. He never shied away from a good fight. He sensed that the media loved one, and he had concluded that the public usually benefits from any airing of all the facts.

He never had any trouble making up his mind, and you were never left with any doubts as to where he stood. George

Fingold and I were political allies from the day we met until his untimely death in 1958 at the age of 50.

I risked my all in a campaign for Congress in 1956, against a longtime incumbent for whom neither George nor I had much respect. He knew better than I that the chance of upsetting an incumbent in a primary was slight, but he was even more enthusiastic than I in taking on the race. We both thought I had a good chance to win.

When I lost the campaign in September of 1956, and we met at a speaking engagement at a school in Dedham, he asked me: "What are you going to do now?"

"Practice law, I guess."

"Come in and see me in the morning." He quickly swore me in as an Assistant Attorney General, and placed me in charge of writing opinions upon behalf of the Commonwealth of Massachusetts – and I was only a few years out of law school! I was flattered by his confidence in me.

The first legal question placed before me was no small matter. It involved the collapse of a bridge that was under construction over the Neponset River at Quincy – and the failure was all over the newspapers. What caused it? Who is liable for the enormous costs?

I was painfully aware of the monstrous sums involved and the likelihood that the contractor had made large campaign contributions to all the politicians involved – including probably one to my boss!

It would have been easy and politic to rule that accidents happen to everyone and that the state should pay a reasonable extra charge. But one line in the lengthy contract read: "This contract is subject to all the rules and regulations of the Massachusetts Department of Public Works." I read that small volume carefully.

Clearly, the contractor was on notice that the state contracted for and expected a usable end product – for the total sum agreed.

Attorney General Fingold stuck his head in the door while I was completing this fascinating research:

"How do you see it?" The press was badgering him for a ruling.

I dreaded a difference of opinion with a man I much admired.

"The contractor is liable... The rules of the DPW entitle us to a usable bridge – at the contract price."

Fingold never hesitated: "If that's the way you see it – that's the way we are going to go."

I have not known many people who could equal that for courage and integrity!

*   *   *   *

The Attorney General paid me a nice compliment when he announced for Governor in 1958: "I want you to introduce me on TV."

What did I have going for me? Young, World War 2 veteran, conspicuous record in the House. But I don't think those are what persuaded Fingold to place some of his fate in my hands.

I think he felt that the Republican party was still dominated by old Yankee families – and he liked to see an old Protestant name on the line with his. The year 1958 was still the era of "talking heads" in television – we had not yet discovered that "sound bites" are cheaper and more persuasive.

George Fingold was on his way to becoming the first Jewish Governor of Massachusetts, and his election was assured. He had earned the support of his own party, and he had a host of friends among Independents and Democrats. But he died suddenly on August 31, 1958 only two months before Election Day – and at the untimely age of 50. No one had expected such a calamity. It turned a sure victory into a sure defeat.

And it had the same result for my second campaign for

Congress in the district that included most of the towns in Norfolk County, plus the cities of Brockton and Quincy. I carried all the towns in the county, plus the city of Brockton, but lost by a few hundred votes in Quincy. A live George Fingold, backing me throughout the district and especially in Quincy, would have made the difference. Governor Herter had intervened in 1956 to preserve his decaying buddy; Governor-to-be Fingold would have intervened in 1958 to put me over.

C'est la guerre...

The Commonwealth was stunned by such an untimely end to such a spectacular career. We named the State Library on the third floor of the State House "the George Fingold Library." A bronze bust of him was created to greet you at the door. The library was an appropriate tribute because George had risen from dire poverty to great public service through dedication to education. He was a product of books – and libraries.

But if you ask for the Fingold Library today, you get blank stares. The young staff never heard of George Fingold. Their library is once again – The State Library.

But an efficient reference desk can find the dates for you. Born in Boston on November 18, 1908. Died in Concord on August 31, 1958.

A great life.

LAW OFFICES

FINGOLD, ROGOVIN & FINGOLD
MIDDLESEX COUNTY BANK BUILDING
ONE SALEM STREET, MALDEN, MASS.

MALDEN 4-5075

GEORGE FINGOLD
MAURICE ROGOVIN
SHIRLEY FINGOLD

June 4, 1951

Hon. Harold Putnam,
315 Warren Street,
Needham 92, Mass.

Dear Harold:-

      I have been more than compensated for the trip I made
to your Town the other night by having some real people, like yourself,
write to me and express their views concerning the present rotten condition we find our Nation and State in. If we could get more citizens,
like Bushnell, to battle the crooked elements, your job and mine would
be made much easier.

      I would be delighted to have you sit in with me on some
trials which may come up that would be of interest to you. However,
our courts close by the end of June and do not re-open until September.

      I trust that your year at Law School was a success and I
am looking forward to the near future when you will, yourself, become
a practicing attorney.

      With kind personal regards, I am

          Sincerely yours,

          George Fingold

GF/MMD

1951 - The author is in law school. George Fingold is en route to being
Attorney General. In 1958, he died after receiving the nomination for
Governor.

Chapter 20

JOHN FITZGERALD KENNEDY – (1917-1963)

John Fitzgerald Kennedy and I were born within a few miles of the State House in Boston. Our birthdays were less than one year apart. We both attended Ivy League colleges.

We both volunteered as Naval officers in World War 2, and after the victories, we both headed for careers in Massachusetts politics.

We were both selected as "Young Men of the Year" by the Greater Boston Junior Chamber of Commerce in 1951.

Jack went on to become a great President. The cornerstones of "Camelot" were laid in those early years.

The future President first came to public attention after his graduation from Harvard, when his father, Joseph, was serving as Ambassador to England and was giving the Roosevelt administration fits by his seeming acceptance of what was going on in Nazi Germany.

His maternal grand-father, John Fitzgerald, was doing more good for Jack's political future by eternal politicking in the City of Boston. In my early years as a cub reporter for The Boston Globe, I used to be dispatched to an occasional political gathering of Irish Catholic Democrats, and always "Honey Fitz" would be the hit of the evening.

His term as Mayor was before my time, but everyone still knew him and liked him. As any meeting wound down to a conclusion, "Honey Fitz" would be champing at the bit to get on the stage and do his thing. He must have been in the 80s around Pearl Harbor time, and he was white-haired and a bit tottery – but he could sing sweetly and with gusto. His "swan song" was "Sweet Adeline."

Old "Fitzie" had begun the Irish-Catholic domination of Boston politics, which continued until an Italian-American managed to achieve the office in present times. The Fitzgerald and Kennedy families nurtured their off-spring to continue the political successes.

Like a good football team, they always had super back-up players. If Joe couldn't do it, then the political manager could send in young Joe. And when young Joe was shot down in the war, then Jack was up next.

And if Jack was not able to do it, there was Bobby. And more enduring than all of the sons was Teddy. Senator Ted has suffered more troubles than most, but the Massachusetts electorate has been willing to forgive his personal foibles.

In 1994, he was re-elected to the Senate, where he has spent his life since meeting the minimum age requirement of 30. He remains probably the most controversial Democrat in national public service, but there is grudging admission now that he has been the most constructive legislator of all the Kennedys.

The Navy released me in March of 1946, and Jack returned to Boston about the same time. The Boston Globe very kindly put me back to work writing a question and answer column, which we called "The Victory Forum" in the early days of the war, and then "The Veterans' Forum" upon my return. Dave Powers, Jack's closest aide, once told me that when they were stuck for an answer to constituents writing to them for help, they always told them to "try The Veterans' Forum."

I don't recall meeting Jack until the spring of 1946. when we were both out of the service, but I had heard about him from City Councilor Clement A. Norton, who was a friend of both of us. Clem saw each of us as rising young politicians, but he was not very favorably disposed toward the Kennedy clan.

Clem was a New Dealer, one of the few in elective office in Massachusetts at the time of the Roosevelt campaign for a third term. Even though Joe Kennedy held important appointments under FDR, Clem knew that on many good causes, Joe was the enemy.

Joseph Kennedy was a graduate of my high school, Boston Latin School, and he was one of the first prominent Irish Catholics to graduate from Harvard College. But he had made a slew of money by questionable means, and he was peculiarly sympathetic to Adolf Hitler during the 1930s. Clem was not inclined to be friendly to the Kennedy clan, and he referred to the young Jack as "The Kid."

Along with "The Kid," I was invited to be a speaker at a rally for the United Nations to be sponsored by the Joint Council for International Co-operation and to be held in Tremont Temple at the foot of Beacon Hill in Boston.

I had helped to organize the Joint Council – an attempt to join all the organizations supportive of international co-operation. President Roosevelt was struggling to launch the United Nations, and community support in the large cities of the country was needed.

We enlisted Mrs. Arthur Rotch, Mrs. Larue Brown, Mrs. Walter E. Dewey and Mrs. Thomas Mahony.

In their younger days, they were the firebrands of feminism who won the right to vote in 1920. They were the organizers of the Women's City Club and other women's groups across the state of Massachusetts. They were the original champions of the National League of Women Voters. And some of them were the loyal friends of Sacco and Vanzetti, victims of the most famous murder case in Massachusetts history.

In 1946, the creation of the United Nations was the great cause of the day, and the Beacon Hill ladies were the leading champions in the Boston area. They wanted to enlist young war veterans in their cause, and Jack and I were with them all the way.

Jack had just announced that he would be a candidate for Congress in the 1946 election, and among all those other pursuits, the Beacon Hill ladies were all New Deal Democrats – prized exhibits of the Democratic pols who were the real powers in the party. It was no accident that they presented him on their program!

But when we arrived to make our speeches, I was surprised to meet another participant on the platform – Bess Myerson, the reigning Miss America! I never knew who arranged that, but I doubt that the Beacon Hill ladies thought of her availability or even knew about her keen interest in politics.

Candidate Jack seemed like the cat who swallowed the canary! In the Puritanical life that I led at that time, it never occurred to me that he had any special interest in the female visitor. Candidates were not subject to the sexual scrutiny that seems to obsess the voters and the media today.

Bess Myerson was a Jewish girl from New York City. She was tall, voluptuous, brainy and a good speaker. She was a fascinating addition to our program. I have forgotten what she said – or what any of us said – but Bess was a significant help in getting across our political message. She has had many successes and failures in New York politics in all the years since, but my favorable image of that Boston meeting still lingers.

Jack's reputation as a "womanizer" had not developed in those virgin years. And maybe he was innocent of bringing Bess to Boston for that United Nations rally. Perhaps the elderly ladies of Beacon Hill thought of it all by themselves. But my guess is that Jack thought of it as a shrewd political move and who was I to object! I too was enthralled!

Jack went off to Washington in January of 1947, a newly-elected Member of Congress, and our paths did not cross again until we were both selected by the Greater Boston Junior Chamber of Commerce in 1951 as "Young Men of the Year." Jack was beginning to be noticed in Washington, and I was a State Representative.

I had made the grade by lambasting some massive state highway corruption that led to major changes in Massachusetts politics.

Not the least of the changes was a successful run by Congressman John F. Kennedy for the United States Senate seat of Henry Cabot Lodge, Jr., a considerable victory while two Republicans – Eisenhower and Herter – were running successfully in Massachusetts for President and Governor.

The Kennedy victory seemed to begin at my law school, Boston University. As a law student myself, I sat in the large lecture hall with my fellow students anxiously awaiting the only one-on-one appearance of the candidates for a widely-publicized debate. Here in this hall we had listened with pain to lectures on evidence and Federal taxation – two of my most troublesome subjects in law school – and now we were to be treated to an open fight to the death between the principal candidates for the United States Senate.

"Geez, I don't think Kennedy can do it." Common comments from my friends and classmates.

"Lodge isn't a bad guy, and he brought Ike into the race for President." My two closest buddies – Mel Miller and Bill Deachman – checked the possibilities with me – because I was still a sitting member of the Massachusetts Legislature. None of us had a crystal ball, but we enjoyed the excitement of something this interesting taking place in our lecture hall. It was a lot more stimulating than our usual fare.

Our Dean escorted Lodge and Kennedy down the center isle to thunderous applause. Most of the students were either present or future leaders in their own communities, and there was a feeling that we all had a personal stake in this outcome.

Lodge was tall and handsome – could have been a movie star. His brother actually was. He was the living symbol of Protestant, Republican, Brahminism – of old wealth from the North Shore.

Kennedy was young, almost boyish, handsome enough but

he seemed almost frail by comparison with the sitting Senator. Irish-Catholic Democrat – from new wealth – most of it derived from booze, movies and speculation! What made him think he could topple the Senator?

We hushed with some awe as the speaking began. I remember Lodge as being sonorous, probably speaking from a prepared text, and Kennedy seemed more intense, more passionate – speaking from a minimum of notes. Who won?

It was not so clear after that debate in the fall of 1952. Kennedy was only 35 – he seemed almost boyish up on the Boston University Law School platform. How could a boy defeat an established statesman – especially one who had battled his party to bring General Eisenhower into position to be the next President? There was a full generation of difference between Lodge and Kennedy, and that would prove to be significant to the swarming veterans who would be a major factor in the November election.

Jack won – proving at an early age that no political goal was beyond his grasp. He went off to Washington, and very quickly began to develop a national constituency. He wrote an excellent book, "Profiles in Courage," selecting political heroes that were also my heroes. I wrote him so – and he wrote a nice letter of thanks – inviting me to lunch when I next visited Washington.

When I did get to Washington in 1959 as a legislative counsel to United States Senator Leverett Saltonstall, we began joint efforts with Senator Kennedy upon behalf of the Massachusetts fishing industry. Despite a difference in party and religion, the Senators worked in harmony on all questions relating to their home state.

The fishing industry was in trouble, and the Senators came up with several suggestions to help it. But the industry was not very good at listening and not very faithful in observing sound marketing and conservation provisions. It is paying for its obstinacy today – the most prolific waters on the eastern seaboard are just about fished out. It will take some patient years before they are

𝔘nited 𝔖tates 𝔖enate
WASHINGTON, D. C.

February 13, 1956

Dear Harold:

Many thanks for your very kind letter. I
appreciate both your good wishes and your generous
comments on my new book "Profiles in Courage. "

If you are ever in Washington I hope you will
come by my office and perhaps we can have lunch
together.

Again many thanks and with every good wish.

Sincerely,

Jack

John F. Kennedy

Hon. Harold Putnam
House of Representatives
State House
Boston, Massachusetts

able to restore themselves.

John Fitzgerald Kennedy was elected President of the United States in November of 1960. His Inauguration was held at the Capitol in January, during the worst blizzard that I have ever seen hit Washington. The city was blanketed with snow, and the roads were glare ice.

I had tried to drive home through Rock Creek Park, and had had to give up. I pulled my car off the road into a snow bank and abandoned it in favor of a ride in a big Navy bus – that was still able to make it to civilization. I reached home all right, but the next day when I went to rescue my car I found a police tag on it – for "Parking on the Grass."

On Inauguration Day, I was among the throng that stood in the snow on the east side of the Capitol. We could hardly see the speakers' platform, and we were shivering with cold. The poet, Robert Frost, had an early spot on the program.

His hair was now snowy white and he seemed very aged – this was twenty-four years after I had sat at his feet in the Baker Library at Dartmouth College and listened to him read his works. He had trouble getting started. He couldn't see his words. He couldn't hold his notes in the freezing cold and blustering winds. It was a Camelot touch for Jack to put a poet on the Inaugural program, and I regretted that the reading had not worked out better.

Before and after the inauguration, would-be appointees came to Washington – seeking a role in what promised to be an exciting and constructive administration. One of my friends – Phil David Fine of Boston – came to me. I was then working in the Senate Small Business Committee offices in the old Senate Office Building – high-ceiling, thick rugs, huge conference table, and around the vast room a few desks for key staff members.

I knew Phil from law school days, and I knew that he was interested in politics:

"What brings you to Washington?", I asked.

"Looking for a job."

"What do you want to do?"

"I'm not that fussy. What do you think might be available?"

I was not that close to the Kennedy hiring team, based at the White House, but my Committee was interested in who would head the Small Business Administration, and we knew that that appointment had not been made.

"Any interest in small business?"

"Sure. I guess so." Phil was lawyer for some of the Loew interests in Boston, and was much involved in the growth of the Patriots football franchise and the construction of their stadium in Foxboro.

"What did you do during the campaign?" I knew that JFK and his "Irish Mafia" had catalogued their friends and enemies more carefully than any other Administration in my lifetime. They knew their friends, and they were now in a position to reward them.

"I ran the President's campaign in New York State," replied Phil.

"Wow! You should be able to get anything that you ask for... I'd get right down to the White House, and make your wishes known."

Phil was gone less than twenty-four hours. He came back beaming: "I got it... Head of the Small Business Administration."

Phil's appointment was characteristic of much that JFK did. The people had given him the power to govern, and he was ready and qualified to use it. There was a sense of purpose and progress in the Kennedy Administration, and it began with making prompt and sound decisions.

* * * * *

Few people working in Washington during the Kennedy Administration were aware of the boiling hatred that was swirling around him behind the scenes in Washington and in some corners of the country. Those of us from Massachusetts, who had known the family and the President for several generations, could understand philosophical differences, but we were not prepared for violent actions.

We know now that at the top of the list of the haters were J. Edgar Hoover, the head of the FBI; the leaders of the CIA, whose blunders infuriated the President; and the southern cracker politicians, who never forgave the Kennedy brothers for their decency to the Rev. Martin Luther King, Jr., and all blacks.

Now, in the 1990s, more than thirty years after Jack's assassination, some interesting facts are beginning to emerge about those who must share the guilt for the tragedy – especially about J. Edgar Hoover.

He had the audacity to try to blackmail the Rev. Martin Luther King, Jr. into silence by critiquing and revealing his private life on the road, while keeping secret his own more unorthodox practices. But the secrets emerged in the 1980s and 1990s, when the few knowledgeable people summoned the courage to speak out about the F.B.I. Director long after his death.

One of the first to suggest strange goings-on was Xavier Hollander in one of her "Happy Hooker" books way back around 1980: "A call came in to go to a New York hotel room. When I entered the room I was dumb-founded to see that my Johns were two of the highest law enforcement officials in the country." They were not interested in Xavier's customary services! We are still waiting for her to tell us who they were!

Further, throughout his reign in Washington, J. Edgar insisted that there was no such thing as the "Mafia" or the "Costra Nostra." Didn't exist, he said, and no agents were assigned to find out if it did. Yet he attended races with dubious characters, and accepted tickets that paid off big on fixed races.

Looking back now upon the November 22, 1963 shooting in Dallas, one has to ask: "Which powerful element in our society hated JFK the most?" High on the list would be what president

Eisenhower called "The military/industrial complex."

Kennedy had decided in October to withdraw from the Vietnam entanglement. He formalized his decision in National Security Action Memorandum 263, which was issued on October 11, 1963 – according to Secretary Robert McNamara and movie director Oliver Stone. The word from the White House reached the military planners in Honolulu on November 20 and 21, 1963 – yet the records of that conference are still classified, despite the 1992 mandate from Congress that all government agencies come clean on whatever they had about the JFK assassination.

Who benefits from government secrecy thirty-plus years after the fact? Who is determined at this late date that the truth shall not come out? Who benefitted from the drastic turn-around in American policy in Vietnam after President Kennedy was buried?

I doubt that we will ever know the details of the assassination that devastated the country in November of 1993. But those of us who have studied the case will never be convinced that one man did it. We will always believe that a sinister conspiracy was carried out by professionals.

The government is still keeping secret massive amounts of information about the Kennedy assassination. (Senator Daniel Moynihan of New York, member of the Senate Intelligence Committee, on CBS "Sixty Minutes," October 19, 1997.) Thirty-four years after the crime! Why?

My special regret is that Chief Justice Earl Warren, well-trained in the law and an experienced criminal prosecutor, let all the incriminating evidence percolate under the surface of government without being exposed. He presided on the bench of the United States Supreme Court when I was admitted to its bar – I expected more of him!

News of the Dallas killing reached Washington early on a Friday afternoon, when I was en route to the Washington airport for a week-end trip to Boston. Go or not go? The love of my life was waiting for me in Boston, and so were some clients. I had no immediate tasks in Washington, and decided to go and then to return early.

When I got back the President's remains were lying in State in the Capitol, just below my office which was up near the dome. The line of mourners stretched several blocks to the east of the Capitol – some remaining in line all night. I was out of the country at the death of FDR, so never before in my lifetime had I seen such an outpouring of public adoration.

For the solemn march to the Arlington Cemetery, special buses were provided for distinguished foreign guests and for members of Congress My boss, former Speaker Joseph W. Martin, Jr., was too feeble to make the trip, but I had hopes for my teen-age daughters, who were with me.

"Fishbait" Miller, the popular Sergeant at Arms of the House, was in charge of loading the buses, and even though he came from Mississippi, he seemed to have a special affection for Mr. Martin:

"Fishbait, you seem to have some extra space on the bus… Any chance of getting me and my girls on there?" I asked.

He didn't hesitate: "Just slip on there quickly."

When the bus arrived at Arlington Cemetery, we pulled up behind the bus discharging the heads of state from all over the world: President Charles DeGaulle of France, Emperor Haile Selassie of Ethiopia, Prince Philip of England, and many others.

Every few years, we see the archival films of the heads of state marching up the Arlington Cemetery hill to stand at the eternal flame over the Kennedy grave. Those teen-age girls interspersing the foreign statesmen are mine.

Jack was different! It hardly seems possible now that more than thirty years have passed since he was snatched away from us. The domestic violence that seemed to target only the Kennedys in the 1960s now targets almost everyone. The good feeling that was beginning to develop between the races now seems as bad or worse than ever.

Once there was a "Camelot." Jack and Jackie gave us a brief image of a "city on a hill", of a castle in the clouds, of a dream that made us proud. We are the worse for their departure.

The Camelot myth was no accident. It was nurtured by the most skilled journalists and historians that Jack Kennedy could lure into public service. From the beginning of his political career, Jack seemed determined both to make history and to write it.

Pierre Salinger crafted the daily news. Ted Sorenson made sure that the speeches were phrased to send some words down through the ages. And Arthur Schlesinger, Jr., was always on hand to observe and record the events of the day with an eye to history.

Arthur's dad had been the Chairman of the Department of History at Harvard College, and Arthur Jr. came from the same fine mold – a distinguished professional and also a fine writer. Arthur Senior was remembered in Boston as a champion of civil rights and freedom of speech. When the City of Boston banned an appearance by Margaret Sanger to speak on birth control, the Harvard Professor mounted the platform of Ford Hall Forum and read the speech!

Young Arthur first appeared on the Boston political scene around 1940, when both us came to the support of an unusual young lady named Frances Sweeney, who formed a Committee to combat anti-Semitism and other hatreds under-currenting the pre-war years in Massachusetts. He seemed to me at the time too scholarly and aloof for usefulness in the daily struggles, but Jack Kennedy seems to have had a clearer vision and a better under-standing of the usefulness and the potential of Arthur Schlesinger, Jr. Schlesinger's writings, perhaps more than anything else, will perpetuate Jack's place in history.

I am less clear about the role of writer Richard Goodwin, later married to Doris Kearns, but surely no couple has done more to glamorize and perpetuate the history of the Kennedy and later the Johnson years than they.

So – where will history place John F. Kennedy in our pantheon of Presidents? It is too early to make that assessment probably, and there is too much interest in these times in the trivia and not enough concern with the long struggles of human history.

But he stood tall in my lifetime. I think he will stand tall in history!

Chapter 21

LEVERETT SALTONSTALL (1892-1979)

Leverett Saltonstall was descended from one of the oldest and richest families in history.

Before I knew him he had been a graduate of Harvard College (Class of 1914 – his license plate number throughout most of his life!), a member of a championship Harvard crew, the Speaker of the Massachusetts House of Representatives and the Governor of Massachusetts.

When I became a cub reporter for The Boston Globe in 1937, my city room associates intrigued me with tales of the goings on in the office building across Devonshire Street in Boston. They claimed those fifth floor rooms across from us were the counting houses of Leverett Saltonstall and other old Boston families.

The desks of our neighbors were only about sixty feet from ours, and after 5 p.m. they offered some interesting sights. Sun-shaded gnomes sat on high stools and made book-keeping entries by hand. We imagined that they were keeping track of the Saltonstall, Cabot and Lodge money, and they were doing it in much the same way that characters did it in the novels of Charles Dickens. One of those 1937 gnomes could have been the grand-son of Dickens' "Scrooge."

After 5 p.m. one evening, we observed that one male and one female had stayed late. Our youthful minds jumped quickly to the interesting possibilities, and we were not to be disappointed.

Male and female came together. Male and female kissed. Male and female began to shed clothing. Our little group of fascinated reporters began to grow as the action heated up.

One clever fellow suggested that we carefully examine the names on the door across the street, and them give the couple a call. He read off the letters, slowly deciphering the backward sign.

Quickly we checked the phone book. There was such a firm, and it was located on Devonshire Street!

We watched the intensifying action and prepared to call. We wanted the harsh ring of the phone to coincide exactly with the moment of penetration. The approach to the desk-top lady, the ring, the consternation, the reluctant pick-up.

And then my "dirty trick" friend applied the coup de grace – in a deep voice that seemed to echo from a sepulcher –:

"This is God calling. Aren't you - - - ashamed?"

I don't recall if I ever told that story to Senator Saltonstall after he hired me in 1958 to be his Minority Counsel to the United States Senate Small Business Committee.

Probably would have been just as well if I did not – he would have considered it a frivolous activity for men who should have been engaged in more serious pursuits. But probably he would have added an old Yankee chuckle.

I had known the Senator for several years as "the man with the South Boston face," – an epithet that James Michael Curley of Boston has hurled at him in a previous campaign, thereby assuring his re-election forever!

He had known me as a younger member of the Legislature in the 1950s, and he had noted my selection as a "Young Man of the Year" in 1951 and had approved my graduation from Law School while serving in the House. And I had discussed with him my decision to run for Congress in 1956.

"But can you afford it," he asked. In the naiveté of my early years that question had never occurred to me! Experience, education, family, goals – all those had seemed pertinent to me, but if my ancestors had been asked that question during the eleven generations before me in the western world, they never would have won anything... And they DID win often, because 58 members of my family had served in the Massachusetts Legislature before me – beginning in the 1600s, when the "General Court" first met.

I ignored his serious question, which was based upon his lifetime of hard experience. And I lost for the lack of about one thousand dollars! I learned to my sorrow that the biggest spender usually wins. The Senator had known that all along... And the campaign funding scandal has become far worse in the many years since the 1950s.

Charles W. Colson, later of Watergate infamy, was on the Senator's staff in 1959, and he actually made the arrangements to bring me to Washington. Jonathan Moore was also on the staff at that time, and he later became Director of the Kennedy School of Government at Harvard University. I had worked with Jonathan's dad, Charles, at The Boston Globe before he left for an important position with the Ford Motor Company. Small world!

During those early days in Washington the Senator was impressed with my letter-writing. About three hundred letters a day piled into his office – two or three deserving of his personal attention, about twenty that were candidates for my answers and his signatures, and the rest to be parceled out to staff specialists.

He used to call me into his office regularly at 9 a.m., and he would review the chores for the day... And then at 4 p.m., he would call me in again, and we would review what we had accomplished – the most methodical leader I ever worked for... But one day he had a special comment!

"Harold," he began, "you write fine letters, but I have one suggestion."

"Yes, sir!"

"Quite often you write: 'The Senator will do everything he can to assist you...' I have found it prudent to write: 'The Senator will do everything *he properly can* to assist you.'"

Long years in public service had convinced him to be cautious about written promises that might survive to haunt him!

I was with the Senator in 1963 and 1964 when the hottest issue of the day was civil rights. I had been one of the leaders in the Massachusetts House in the 1950s when we pushed through legislation creating a Fair Employment Practices Commission, the Massachusetts Commission Against Discrimination, and forbidding discrimination in public housing.

I had helped with the earliest campaigns of Edward W. Brooke, whom we later advanced to the United States Senate – the only black male ever to be elected by popular vote to that body. So Melnea Cass, the matriarch of the black community in Boston, was an old friend of mine.

She led a Massachusetts delegation into the Senator's office in 1964 to plead for his support for the key civil rights bill. And she "talked turkey." Bill Saltonstall, the Senator's son, and I stood in the back of the room listening.

"Senator," Mrs. Cass was saying. "This is not just a routine visit. We have been with you many times before. Most of us have supported you all during your political life, and now we expect you to support us.

"This pending bill is crucial to our equal rights. And you hold a crucial vote… We don't want the bill defeated by partisanship… And we don't want any more surrendering to bigotry… Enough is enough!"

Bill leaned over and whispered to me: "Geez. Nobody ever spoke like that to my father before."

The bill passed, and the Senator voted for it!

* * * * *

The funniest thing that ever happened to me in the Senator's office developed from a letter about "fish flour."

A letter came in from Ezra Levin, President of the Viobin Corporation of Champagne, Illinois. He owned a fish processing plant in New Bedford in our state, and he was fuming against the

Food & Drug Administration for banning human consumption of "fish flour."

I took the letter seriously. When I called it to the Senator's attention, he thought it was a joke. For weeks afterwards, he would tease me about it:

"How we doing with fish flour?"

The truth was we were doing pretty well. At least I was making some progress. I knew that Ezra Levin was for real – he headed a thriving company and his wife was a leader of the League of Women Voters in Illinois.

He was making "fish flour" out of "trash fish" – including heads and tails. He used a secret process involving a type of alcohol that was toxic but, it seemed to be working. He expected his fish flour to feed the hungry masses of the world!

But George Larrick, the Director of the FDA, had two major objections:

1. The process used the whole fish – not just the filets, and
2. The processing chemical was unacceptable, even though there was no evidence of it remaining in the finished product.

I checked with Senator Paul Douglas of Illinois. He knew Ezra Levin and he would support him and his controversial product.

The two Senators agreed to invite Mr. Larrick to lunch at a private Senate dining room, and secretly we agreed that some of Levin's "fish flour" would be incorporated in everything served at lunch – in the rolls and in the entree.

Things went pleasantly – until Mr. Larrick was told the awful truth... Then he refused to take another bite. He still opposed the use of the whole fish, and he still opposed the chemical process.

For years later the government passed out millions of dollars to major universities and chemical companies, asking them to come up with a process that would produce a satisfactory finished product without using any toxic chemical. When I last checked, no one had been able to produce a result as good as Mr. Levin's and fish flour is still not approved for human consumption in the U.S.A.

Ezra Levin of the VioBin Corporation of Champagne, Illinois, was a nutrition prophet not fully appreciated in his own time. Not even I had full confidence in his unique genius.

When I came down with an unexpected heart attack in 1966, Mr. Levin shipped a quart bottle of Vitamin E to my hospital bedside. I didn't know what to do with it. No doctor had ever considered Vitamin E to be helpful in the treatment of heart disease. Without a doctor's prescription, I didn't dare take it.

But now – thirty years later – what is high on the list of vitamins most respected for keeping arteries open? Vitamin E!

Mr. Levin was a prophet who was a generation ahead of his time – on fish flour and upon Vitamin E. The Congressional mail does not turn up many citizens like Ezra Levin, but when it does we'd better pray that some staffer and some Senator will read it with the respectful attention that it deserves.

I left the Senator's staff in the mid-1960s to return to Massachusetts, and to help elect then Attorney General Edward W. Brooke to the United States Senate upon the retirement of Senator Saltonstall. Once Brooke faced down the possible competition from Governor John A. Volpe his election was assured.

And upon his election, he insisted that new President Richard Nixon, name me the New England Regional Director of the United States Department of Health, Education and Welfare. Brooke would approve no one else, and eventually the White House acquiesced.

But not until retired Senator Saltonstall put in a good word for me also. I knew he was making a trip to Washington in the fall of 1969, so I asked him to speak to Bob Finch, the California lieutenant of Nixon who was then the Secretary of the HEW Department.

He did – and when he returned I asked:

"What did Finch say?"

He said. "Keep your pecker up." That sounded strange from my Puritanical Senator – but by Watergate we had become accustomed to crude language from the Nixon White House.

82 DEVONSHIRE STREET, ROOM 608
BOSTON, MASSACHUSETTS 02109

NOV 20 19

Department of

November 19, 1968

Honorable Harold Putnam
Assistant Attorney General
State House
Boston, Massachusetts

Dear Harold:

The Leslie Cutler dinner which you
organized and at which you presided was
the best affair of that t pe that I have
ever attended. I am confident that the
objective of the dinner was to give Leslie
a good time, and I am sure she had it.
She was mighty pleased not only with the talks
but with the gifts that she received.

Altogether she had many more activities
than I had ever realized, and she can be very
proud of what she has done and with the respect with which people hold her.

With best regards, I am,

Sincerely yours,

Leverett Saltonstall

LS/aw

**1968 - All the important leaders in Massachusetts turned out for a
"This Is Your Life" dinner for State Senator Leslie B. Cutler of
Needham. Senator Saltonstall and Mrs. Cutler knew each other as
children residing on Commonwealth Avenue in Boston.**

Chapter 22

SPEAKER JOE MARTIN (1884 – 1968)

During the last half of the twentieth century my home state of Massachusetts seemed to have a lock on the office of Speaker of the House.

In the forty years from 1947 to 1987, three Congressmen from Massachusetts held the office of Speaker for a combined total of twenty-three years: Joe Martin for four, John McCormack for nine and Tip O'Neill for ten. They came from different parties, supported different philosophies and had different temperaments, but they all served with distinction and they were all my friends.

Joseph W. Martin, Jr., was born in North Attleboro, Massachusetts, in 1884, edited the local newspaper, was elected Congressman in 1924 and served for forty years. He was the Speaker of the House from 1947 to 1949, in the Truman years, and again from 1953 to 1955, at the peak of Eisenhower's power.

He was "Mr. Republican" from the New Deal years until his defeat in 1966. He was the Chairman of every Republican convention from 1940 to 1958.

When James Milne retired as his Administrative Assistant in 1963, after nearly forty years with the Speaker, Mr. Martin asked me to take over the duties and set me up in palatial offices right at the base of the dome of the Capitol. Staff whose duty it was to fly countless flags over the Capitol – so Congressmen could ship them to their constituents – had to go right past my door.

I was a little surprised when the Speaker turned to me. My

political views were considerably more liberal than his, but so were the views of thousands of new voters just added to his district in Wellesley, Needham and Newton – affluent suburbs to the southwest of Boston.

One of the first invitations from his new constituents came from Newton and from Jerome Grossman, whose father had been a fund-raiser for Boston Mayor James Michael Curley and who had inherited his dad's love of politics. But Jerry was even more successful than his father – highly intelligent, deeply concerned about serious issues and a genius at political organizing. Later he became the Democratic National Committeeman for Massachusetts, and the creator of Congressman and priest, Robert Drinan, who initiated the motion to impeach Richard Nixon!

I brought the letter in to the Speaker, first with a suggestion and then with advice on the reply:

"Mr Speaker. I know Mr. Grossman and the city of Newton. This is a very important part of your district now. This will be a house meeting – but there will be about twenty smart people there. I think they need to know you. I suggest that you accept."

I would not have been surprised if he had suspected a trap, and if he had looked for an excuse to reject the invitation. But -

"If you think we ought to go, OK. Let's do it."

The meeting went about as I expected. We were in the middle of the Vietnam war, and Newton was a hot-bed of opposition. And Jerry Grossman was the spokesman. The introductions made and the pleasantries spoken Jerry zeroed in on the Congressman – now over 80 and physically feeble.

"Mr. Speaker. Many of us are strongly opposed to the Vietnam war, and the way President Johnson is keeping it going. We would like to hear your views."

I wondered how Mr. Martin would handle the "hot potato." He was a generation older than I, and I had not yet felt sufficiently close to him to discuss controversial questions. But he had not been in politics for more than four decades without learning how to handle hostile questions.

"I don't mind telling you how I feel about Vietnam," he replied without hesitation. "I never was for that war anyway. I wish we had never gone in there."

But this was no ordinary group of constituents. The questions continued:

"But, Mr. Speaker, you keep voting for the funds to keep the war going. Your votes don't show much opposition."

"Perhaps so," he replied calmly. "I am not prepared to let down the troops that we have out there now. But I assure you that I will do what one Congressman can do to end the whole sorry mess."

Joe Martin made some friends that night. Even those who disagreed with his usually conservative views were charmed by his candor and concern. Other keen observers of national politics usually reacted to Mr. Martin in the same way.

Across many a banquet hall, Clarence Mitchell, the Washington lobbyist for the NAACP. would often see me and interrupt his speech to relay a sincere word of appreciation to Mr. Martin. Although the Speaker was never known in his home district as a champion of civil rights, he had done something crucial and significant that produced the Civil Rights Act of 1964 – and Clarence Mitchell was eternally grateful.

Some of the Speaker's other friends were three of the world's most renowned ladies: Clare Booth Luce, playwright, publisher's wife, one-time Congresswoman and one-time Ambassador; Madame Chiang Kai-Shek, wife of the Generalissimo of the old China; and Madame Chennault, the wife of the "Flying Tiger" General in World War 2. All of these ladies made a pilgrimage to Speaker Martin's office whenever they came to the Capitol.

Probably they were attracted originally to political power. But the friendships seemed to endure for better reasons. They enjoyed reliving the good old days of the 1950s, when Ike was in the White House and all seemed right with the world.

Joe was a bachelor all his life, and there was some amusement that these three famous ladies were his frequent guests. But I do not recall any preoccupation then with a political leader's sex life, such as seems to grip the press and the public today.

A person's sexual preferences were his own business. It didn't seem to make any difference at the polls whether a candidate was married or unmarried. Actually, a bachelor seemed to have some advantages, when once elected – no wifely demands, no children's needs, no complaints about working nights or long trips.

A bachelor could stay in the office well into the evening – even go to work on Saturdays and Sundays – all of which Mr. Martin did often. Politics was his whole life, and public service was his first and only love.

The wife of Justice Oliver Wendell Holmes, Jr., once said: "Washington is full of great men, and the women they married in their youth." Joe Martin never had to worry about that problem.

The Speaker and I both kept a political eye on what was going on back in Massachusetts. We were aware that the rising star in the early 1960s was the new Attorney General, Edward W. Brooke – the first black ever to be elected in our home state to statewide office.

We had a request one day for Brooke to speak, and I relayed it back to him at the State House in Boston:

"Ed. Mr. Martin would like to have you fill a speaking engagement at the Lincoln Day Dinner of the Baltimore Republican Club. Can you do it?"

Brooke was not anxious to leave Massachusetts for an out-of-state affair. I tried to make it easy for him.

"If you will fly into Washington, Speaker Martin will make his limousine and chauffeur available to you for the evening."

The elongated Cadillac limousine, complete with uniformed chauffeur, was one of the nicest "perks" of being an ex-

Speaker of the House, and Mr. Martin was very generous with it. Many constituents were given guided tours of Washington in the limousine – and they are still talking about it!

"OK," Brooke finally replied, "but only on the condition that you write a suitable speech for me." Agreed.

Lincoln was one of my favorite Presidents and Brooke was my favorite among the younger politicians coming along in Massachusetts, so it was not difficult for me to draft a stirring oration.

Weeks later, on the day after Lincoln's birthday, the chauffeur came into my office for his limousine assignments for the day.

"How'd the Brooke speech go in Baltimore," I asked, expecting him to rave about my immortal words.

"Terrific," he replied. "He wowed them. And all he used were a few notes on the back of an envelope."

* * * * * *

Speaker Martin was over 80 during that last term in the House from 1964 to 1966.

One could detect the signs of the creeping loneliness of old age. When Justice Louis D. Brandeis was about the same age, I had heard him say wistfully: "Most of my friends are gone now."

Not only the loneliness was a problem, but also the physical infirmities of old age – an urinary problem, difficulty in walking. He could not get around without the limousine and his patient chauffeur.

One siege of illness took him to the Bethesda Naval Hospital, where he was lodged in a "Tower Suite" – always reserved for Presidents and occasionally for slightly lesser dignitaries.

The accommodations were palatial, but the patient was largely unvisited and forgotten. I spent several evenings with Mr. Martin and never encountered any other visitors.

He brightened when we talked politics, especially about Wendell Willkie, and the Republican national campaign that Joe managed in 1940.

"I liked Willkie," he said. "He was a real leader and a good speaker." I had known Joe to go through the motions loyally for some horrible Republican candidates. He had obviously been relieved to have had a candidate as appealing as Willkie.

We talked on through the evening – an oral history lesson for me. He had known all the Presidents since Woodrow Wilson. He was the champion of General Douglas MacArthur. He was really the personification of small-town America. But that is to say a lot of good about the man.

As I rose to leave the hospital room, I could not help but think that for bachelors and for the childless old age can be a lonely time.

And the approach of death can be a frightening thing – even for the bravest of men. Power and money and votes seemed less important now as the last minutes of life ticked away.

No marble temples have been erected to Speaker Joe Martin. No immutable changes were wrought by him in the laws of the land.

But Joseph W. Martin, Jr. of North Attleboro, Massachusetts, will be remembered as a good and decent man.

Chapter 23

THE FEDERAL YEARS

When Richard M. Nixon was elected President in 1968 and my friend, Edward W. Brooke, was safely in the United States Senate, those of us who had worked in the Republican vineyard for more than twenty years in Massachusetts looked forward to some significant role in the new Administration.

Ed asked me: "What do you want? I think I will have the last say on the Regional Directors – Commerce, Environmental Protection, H.E.W."

I chose the Department of Health, Education and Welfare – most of my legal and legislative experience was in that field. He promised to see what he could do, and I knew from my six years on Capitol Hill that an incumbent Senator could do a lot – when his party occupied the White House. In fact, he usually had the total last word. But an appointment was slow in coming.

Nixon went into office in January of 1969, but any appointment for me was still hanging fire in the closing quarter of the year.

But eventually, in early 1970, the appointment came through. I was the Regional Director of the United States Department of Health, Education and Welfare, with a corner office on the 15th floor of the Kennedy Building in Boston – with Social Security, welfare disbursements, the Public Health Service, the Food and Drug Administration, and a host of other programs under our jurisdiction. Fifteen thousand employees and a budget running up into the billions.

I was a "bureaucrat." I still shudder when I hear citizens using that word disparagingly. I have known some great bureaucrats – employees who would risk their jobs for a principled decision, who genuinely loved serving the public and who were paid less than was available in the private sector. My 1972 salary – when I was the highest paid Federal official in New England – was $39,000. Today CEOs of small hospitals and Superintendents of Schools, even in rural areas, make three times as much.

My first assignment was to go visit the Governors of the six New England states, and try to create a good working relationship. I knew Francis W. Sargent of Massachusetts well – he had been my passenger on at least one week-end trip to Boston from Washington. And I knew and liked Kenneth Curtis of Maine.

Walter Peterson of New Hampshire I had never met, although I had heard that he was a Dartmouth graduate. I walked into his sumptuous office in the Capitol Building in Concord, New Hampshire, and began to introduce myself.

"Oh, I know you," began the Governor. "You got me into politics."

I had no idea why he was saying that.

"You did a telecast in 1958 when you ran for Congress, and we could get that station in Peterborough. You sat on a desk, with your family behind you, and just talked about what you would like to accomplish. I thought that talk was so terrific, I decided to give politics a try… And now look where I am!"

In his retirement years, Walter Peterson is now the interim President of the University of New Hampshire – winding up a very useful career in public service.

Regional Directors had only an occasional relationship with the White House. We did meet with President Nixon there once, and another time at Camp David. And we were continually assured that Federal power was being decentralized to regional offices and to states to bring government closer to the people.

The President sent his chief of staff, John Ehrlichman, to

Boston in Air Force One, to convince us that a new day was about to dawn in the relationship between the White House and the regions. I was quietly skeptical. And in my view, it never happened! The Nixon White House remained in total control.

One regional decision did come down to me, and I was fully appreciative. I could name an Assistant Regional Director for Health , – and I could write the qualifications, interview the candidates and make the selection. And the pay would be only slightly below mine.

Three top health experts applied: Dr. David French, a black M.D. who seemed to know Ed Brooke from boyhood days in Washington, D.C.; Dr. Gertrude Hunter, a black lady M.D. – the only one I ever knew at that time; and William Bronstein, a Brockton, Massachusetts, activist. I interviewed each of them at length and would have been happy with any one of them – they were all superbly qualified. Despite my strong feelings in favor of blacks and women, I chose Bill.

He had sold a business, retired early, and had taken on the almost impossible job of transforming the sad, run-down Brockton Hospital. He had the uncommon notion that the city hospital should be run for the benefit of the citizens and the patients – not the radiologists and the doctors and the rest of the staff.

I watched him almost with disbelief as he talked away at the end of a long table in my office. He was smiling throughout his presentation and very assured. Out of his business and accounting background, he talked programs and figures and results. And he had been fearless in taking a knife to "sacred cows."

I was charmed by his manner and awed by his effectiveness. I had never met a community activist who had achieved such remarkable results. I hired him, but he only lasted a year with me. The Secretary of the Department shared my enthusiasm for Bill and his good works, and offered him a top job in Washington.

Dr. French became the Dean of the Boston University School of Medicine, and later was selected by the Agency for

International Development to create public health departments in each of the West African countries.

And Dr. Hunter became our Regional Director of the U.S. Public Health Service – I think the first black and the first woman to hold such a position in government service. Later she became a professor at the Howard University Medical School.

Perhaps the most important power of a Regional Director was in the control of grants – big money grants to colleges and hospitals. We could not deny them if the criteria were met, but we could hold them up, we could ask questions and we could make recommendations. Sometimes I did all three!

The Dean of Tufts Medical School came to my office, seeking final approval of an important Federal grant. I knew some important things about the school and its finances:

Tufts educates a large percentage of all the dentists in New England.

The earnings of dentists in 1972 topped all other professions.

The donations to Tufts by dentists were pitifully small.

"Dean, I am going to have to approve your grant application, because you meet all the usual criteria," I assured him, "but I want to ask a helpful favor."

"What's that?" He showed some concern.

"I want you to take steps to get more revenue each year from your own alumni."

"We do that," he claimed.

"Well then, you do not do it very well. Your dentists are earning more money than anyone else in New England, and they are giving a pitifully small percentage back to their college – and often none at all."

"What do you suggest?"

"I suggest that you send one of your finance officers up to see how the Dartmouth Alumni Fund does it... After nearly forty years out of college, my class of 1937 shows each year better than a 75% participation and the average gift is around $400... I am guessing that your participation is less than 20% and your average gift is under $100."

He was silent for a moment. I don't think he had ever compared his alumni fund-raising effort with that of other colleges. He did not like the figures that he heard. But he knew they were about right.

He agreed to send a finance officer up to Dartmouth to learn how they do it. I signed the grant. I think he kept his promise. I wonder how Tufts Dental is doing now?

Some of the other grant applications hit even closer to home. One came in from the Faulkner Hospital in the Jamaica Plain section of Boston, which wanted to tear down its old wooden hospital completely and build a large, modern institution on the same site. I could not be more sympathetic. It serviced my old neighborhood of Hyde Park and it saw me through a heart attack recovery in 1966.

But one admission in the application disturbed me. They planned a clinic in Weston, a wealthy suburb that was home to many doctors, but no out-patient service for Jamaica Plain, Dorchester and Hyde Park – heavily populated poorer areas that were right under their noses.

I stalled on signing the grant, and requested a commitment for out- patient services in the near areas of Boston. My boyhood friend, Dr. John Ellis Knight, was the hospital's chief of medical services!

Jack's brother, "Pete," had been my canoe mate on several long trips, and Jack had driven to Burlington, Vermont, in 1933, with our kayak on the top of his car, so that we could begin our around New England trip on Lake Champlain.

I persuaded Jack of the fairness of my request. He agreed that the hospital would provide local out-patient service. And now – 23 years later – I note that there is an out-patient clinic in Cleary Square, Hyde Park!

My third struggle over Federal grants struck even closer to home. It involved my Alma Mater – Dartmouth College. I had to advise President John Kemeny that if Dartmouth wanted to continue receiving Federal grants, it would have to go co-ed! ... This was probably not news to him – the act of Congress made the ruling inevitable. But he and I both knew what a drastic change this would be for the outdoorsy, manly image of dear old Dartmouth.

It has been a struggle for the older alumni to get used to the change, but I suspect now that there are many alumni who would like to start over again! In my day there were about 2000 students to compete for about 20 nurses. Today there are about 4000 students, and the genders are about equal.

Dr. John Kemeny was one of my favorite Dartmouth Presidents. His only short-coming was that he was a chain-smoker and that cost him an untimely death. Before he went to Dartmouth, he was an assistant to Albert Einstein at Princeton, and a genius at mathematics and new ideas. He was the first to install a personal computer beside his Presidential desk, and the first to suggest that libraries ought to be indexed onto computers.

Today students at any of the several libraries on the Dartmouth campus can locate any book in the multi-million collection by typing "find-author-name" or "find-topic-subject." Fantastic!

I made him Chairman of a Regional Director's Advisory Committee, which met periodically around New England. The idea was so successful that the Secretary of H.E.W. picked it up, and required it in the other nine regions around the country.

Some of my employees adapted more readily than others to getting things done. And they complied with my request that they answer all inquiries the day they received them, and with the courtesy and diligence that they would apply for the benefit of their favorite relative!

Dr. Taylor was one of them. He was a division all by himself, and his only duty was to see to the safety of water supplies throughout New England. He was a fine scientist and a devoted public servant, and he saw no conflict between the ideals of both.

He came to me one day with a problem.

"I think I ought to go to Vermont," he explained, "and I should spend about a month up there."

"Why Vermont," I asked – knowing that Vermont was the land of milk and honey and the nearest thing we had in New England to unspoiled nature.

"I think some of their water supplies are in trouble."

"You don't need me... Go ahead."

"Well, my report may cause an explosion, and I just thought you ought to be prepared for it."

Dr. Taylor did write a critical report, not just of a few municipal water supplies, but of contamination of domestic supplies out on some farms in the pristine countryside. But there was no explosion. Vermonters cleaned up their act, and today protect their environment better than any other state in the nation.

Another small division that produced spectacular results with a minimum of personnel was the Regional Office of Surplus Property. They operated with just two professionals – one the seeker and the finder, and the other the attorney to supervise the paper work.

They found " gold mines" all over the country, and our Department was near the top of the list of eligible receivers. If we wanted the stuff and if we could find a good use for it, we could have it.

We found a large piece of Federal property in Framingham, Massachusetts, and held it until the state could agree to take it over. And then we notified the Congressman for the District – Robert Drinan – which I always considered a routine procedure and just common courtesy, regardless of party.

But the White House did not see it that way! Not until years later did we learn that Bob Drinan was on Richard Nixon's "enemy list." Bob had the last word – being the first to recommend impeachment proceedings.

Another time the Surplus Property Office found forty fully-equipped dental offices on the surplus list, and they were located in a supply depot in western Pennsylvania.

Did we want them? Could we find uses for them? How would we get them to Massachusetts, and elsewhere in New England?

One of my assistants had cultivated a good relationship with the Massachusetts National Guard. We urged them to improve their public relations by being the ever-ready helper in community service. They have both the manpower and the equipment to undertake major assignments. Would they go and fetch this surplus equipment?

Would they then deliver it to forty different locations throughout New England, if we selected the schools and charities most in need of dental equipment? They not only went and picked it up; they installed it!

Sometimes a program will make you a lot of friends – as that dental project did, but sometimes one will make you a lot of enemies. I made the enemies in the Associated General Contractors of Massachusetts by agreeing to speak to their annual meeting in Boston.

They needed a lecture on affirmative action, and I was angry enough with them to deliver it. And Regional Engineer James Sullivan was brave enough to arrange the invitation and to accompany me. We both knew that the construction industry had a sorry record of age-old discrimination against both blacks and women.

I appealed to their Christian charity. I appealed to their American principles of equal treatment under the law. I appealed to their basic fairness. I knew their sorry record cold, and I knew that the Governor of Massachusetts and the Massachusetts Commission Against Discrimination supported the position that I was taking. And I make a better speech when I am a little angry.

Yankee Journal

ROBERT F. DRINAN
3D DISTRICT, MASSACHUSETTS

509 CANNON HOUSE OFFICE BUILDING
PHONE: 202-225-5931

COMMITTEES:
JUDICIARY
HOUSE INTERNAL SECURITY

DISTRICT OFFICES:
76 SUMMER STREET
FITCHBURG, MASSACHUSETTS 0142(
PHONE: 617-342-8722

400 TOTTEN POND ROAD, BLDG. 1
WALTHAM, MASSACHUSETTS 0215(
PHONE: 617-890-9455

Congress of the United States
House of Representatives
Washington, D.C. 20515

October 2, 1972

Mr. Harold Putman,
    Regional Director
Department of Health, Education
    and Welfare
J.F.Kennedy Federal Building
Government Center
Boston, MA

Dear Harold:

I send to you my deep appreciation for your characteristic thoughtfulness and kindness in inviting me to the ceremony at which the Federal-State land was turned over to the Town of Framingham.

I wish that you and your Department had jurisdiction over other land in my Congressional District which I am seeking to reacquire from the Pentagon!

I take this occasion also to thank you for the countless kindnesses which you have extended to me and to Bill Flynn.

With best wishes to Glendora and with warm personal regards, I am

Cordially yours,

Robert F. Drinan
Member of Congress

RFD:se

1972 - Only one year later than this routine land transfer, the President fired the author, and this Congressional courtesy was a likely factor. A short time later, Father Drinan filed the original impeachment proceedings against Nixon.
(Later revelation - Congressman Drinan was on the White House "enemies list.")

"Geez," Jim Sullivan exclaimed when I came down from the platform. "You really gave it to them." He had never heard me make a formal speech before, and he was quite impressed.

But the White House was not impressed. I heard from them immediately. We know now that the Associated Contractors were big contributors to Nixon, and their wishes received a high priority. My call came from John Venniman, the No. 2 in command of our Department, behind Elliot L. Richardson.

I knew and liked John Venniman, and had noted that he had more social conscience than I expected in a Nixon lieutenant. I suspected the purpose of his call. He was a little apologetic for having to make it!

"The White House is burned up about your speech to the contractors."

"Oh. Both the state and we have a lot of construction going on out there, and Governor Sargent is with me on this."

"Can't help it… The White House orders that you not get into this any further."

I refrained – reluctantly. I had done all that I could do. A little progress has been made in the many years since.

A happier story is how we sent all the poor kids in Massachusetts to two-weeks of residential summer camp. This was the kind of project that had my enthusiastic support, because I spent all the summers of my youth at a boys' camp, and I loved every minute of it.

The missionary who insisted upon seeing me about this matter was a fellow named Ed Johnson. I don't recall knowing him very well, and I am not sure of his affiliation, but I think he represented the American Camping Association. And I wonder now if he was related to the financial genius of the same name who founded Fidelity Investments.

Ed called my attention to some quirk in a Federal appropriation that allowed Regional Directors to spend money to send poor kids to summer camp – provided that the states appropriated an equal amount.

"If you can get Speaker Bartley to go along, we can send something like 200,000 kids to camp." He convinced me – and I was willing to give it a try.

We only had a few days to complete the financing, and then only a week or two to get the word out to the local governments and charities that would find and sign up the kids. I headed up the hill to the Massachusetts State House.

Speaker Bartley came into the Legislature after my time, so I had never met him. But we had mutual friends who were still there, and he had had a good report about me.

I got down to business immediately. "Mr. Speaker. We have an unique opportunity to send every poor kid in Massachusetts to summer camp for two weeks, but we have to move quickly.

"If you can put up about a million dollars, I can make another million of Federal funds available. But we only have about forty-eight hours to act."

I embellished my plea with a report upon my own camp days, and some figures about the benefit of getting these kids off the streets and into a healthy outdoor environment. He did not need any convincing.

He smiled his complete agreement. "I'll do my best, and I think I can wrap it up in two days." He did it – a miracle of legislative efficiency!

All of these constructive miracles came to a crashing end with the re-election of Richard M. Nixon in November of 1972. A few days after the election results were final I had a strange call from my superior Mrs. Pat Hitt: "The President is asking all of his appointees to submit their resignations immediately. Please address it to him at the White House, and send me a copy."

I wasn't surprised. The press had suggested that this strange move was in the works. No President had ever before in all the years of American history requested the resignations of all his appointees. It was an ominous move to centralize all Federal power in the White House – regardless of Congressional mandates as to the duties of Federal agencies.

I didn't have much choice, and I foresaw the move as the beginning of the end for me. Any White House objections seemed petty compared to the constructive and appreciated record that we could show – but the President did not like my lecture on discrimination to the Massachusetts contractors, and he did not like my fair treatment of Congressman Drinan and he probably objected to my presiding over the 50th anniversary of the Community Church of Boston, at which I introduced Roger Baldwin, the President of the American Civil Liberties Union.

But I wrote the letter – as terse and unfriendly as I could make it: "Dear Mr. President: As you requested, I hereby submit my resignation as New England Regional Director of the United States Department of Health, Education and Welfare." Period!

Weeks went by and then Mrs. Hitt called:

"I regret this – but I have to tell you that the President has accepted your resignation."

"Has Senator Brooke approved?"

"Oh, I am sure he has."

I was not so sure. I knew of no reason why Ed would approve. We had had a David and Jonathan relationship for more than twenty years, and friends like that walk into the line of fire for each other. The Brooke family always came to my town for Fourth of July activities, and we always visited the Brookes on Christmas Day. And Ed and I were in almost weekly contact through all those years.

And I had worked on the Hill long enough – for the United States Senate – to know that Senators have absolute control over Federal appointments in their state, at least while a member of their party is in the White House. As to Massachusetts, I was positive that no President would make or break any Leverett

Saltonstall (Brooke's predecessor) recommendation without his knowledge and approval. But my friend Ed was not Saltonstall!

When Brooke and I met, he showed no inclination to resist the White House move. I asked him if I should vent my feelings to the press as I departed – figuring that since he had orchestrated my appointment, he had a right to orchestrate my departure.

"No. I wouldn't do that... It would sound like sour grapes."

Not to me! It would sound like righteous indignation! I had a good relationship with the Boston media, and I knew that they would welcome a public fight with the President! (Massachusetts was the only State that Nixon did not carry in the 1972 landslide). Wise voters in Massachusetts!

Then came another call from Mrs. Hitt: "The President has asked me to call you. He would appreciate a better letter of resignation... You could say you are leaving for a better job."

I paused for a minute, my brain tuning up to high speed. I wasn't about to do the President or his Administration any favors.

"Mrs. Hitt... I can't do that... My mommy told me never to tell a lie... And the truth is there is no prospect of a better job... There is no better job in New England."

Silence on the Washington end of the line. Then: "OK. I'll relay the word."

I have always wondered why my friend, Ed, went along. He must have needed something at the White House desperately – and my head was the price that he had to pay!

For eighteen years I was troubled by the fact that I seemed to be the only Presidential appointee whose resignation was accepted! Why had the President gone to such extreme lengths just to get me? Despite the fact that I read all the autobiographies of other Presidential appointees, no other victim turned up – in all the years from 1973 to 1991.

Then the West Publishing Company printed the autobiography of Erwin N. Griswold, the Dean who had befriended me at

Harvard Law School and the Solicitor General of the United States under both Presidents Johnson and Nixon. If there was ever a model public servant, Dean Griswold was it!

But he too had filed his resignation as requested, and the book reported that it had been accepted! There was a Number Two!

The Dean was always a mild-mannered professional, but he took three pages of his autobiography to excoriate Nixon and his Administration. " Never in my wildest dreams did I imagine that my government would stoop to the shabby activities that I observed in the Nixon White House."

The Solicitor General represents the United States before the Supreme Court. Nixon wanted control of how his friends were treated in pending cases.

Dean Griswold inherited strict Yankee integrity. He was in the way .

I have felt much better about my "resignation" since reading the Griswold autobiography, "Olde Fields; New Corn." I am in the very best of company!

Yankee Journal

Christian Science Monitor - June 1970

'Coatholding' avoided

HEW regional chief called blunt, dedicated

By Jo Ann Levine
Staff writer of The Christian Science Monitor

Boston

"Harold Putnam is straightforward. In fact, for a bureaucrat, he is downright blunt!"

The speaker was one of Mr. Putnam's 2,200 staff members. However, he obviously approved of the new regional administrator of the United States Department of Health, Education, and Welfare who has been so outspoken since June 1, his first day on the job.

Mr. Putnam, for example, has offered to testify against a plan to build a nuclear power plant in Vermont. (The plan formerly had had the benign approval of HEW.) And during a visit to racially tense New Bedford, Mr. Putnam remarked that the black community "wants someone to protect them from their police department. . . . And from the looks of things, I think they are right." His staff explains: "He makes such remarks because he is dedicated."

Candor called gentlemanly

A former assistant attorney general for Massachusetts, and a state representative for eight years, Mr. Putnam is a Nixon administration appointee who is likely to get away with his candor because he is so gentlemanly about it.

But it is obvious that Mr. Putnam has no intention of blending into the anonymous cubbyholes of the John F. Kennedy federal building where he holds a 15th-floor corner office. Nor does he see his job as being a "coatholder." (A "coatholder" is a man who spends most of his time meeting officials at airports, touring them around, and taking them back to the airport.) Mr. Putnam realistically estimates that "coatholding" will take up only about 5 percent of his time.

He has made frequent trips to visit projects representing the $2.5 billion HEW is spending tthis year in New England. He thinks the HEW staff should follow his example.

He also believes that the regional staff should be answerable for the programs it administers. He does not believe in "pass-ing the buck" to Washington, and intends for his staff to "cut it out."

Mr. Putnam said, "HEW is decentralizing . . . and this time it really means it. Soon," he added, "regional offices will be making 80 percent of the decision on grants-in-aid programs."

HEW's regional staff is surprised that Mr. Putnam shows such an interest in "even the smallest details" of their jobs. They assume that after he becomes more familiar with the details he will be less interested in them.

Every Tuesday the top administrators meet for about an hour. This group includes people from the fields of health, education, the Food and Drug Administration, the Social and Rehabilitation Service, and the Office of Civil Rights.

Experience called 'pragmatic'

At one recent meeting, for example, the staff discussed whether: Hartford, Conn., is going to have to drink dirty river water; two Grade 14's will have to share an office; telephone credit cards are going to be canceled.

Mr. Putnam patiently listened while one of his Ph.D. administrators described the HEW summer-intern program as "a very important, meaningful, analytical, pragmatic experience."

Since Mr. Putnam's appointment, his former boss, Elliot L. Richardson, has been promoted to Secretary of HEW. "Every day I served as assistant attorney general," Elliot was attorney general," he said. "It makes my job easy, because I know how Elliot thinks and how he works, and what I can do and can't do — almost without talking to him."

A graduate of Boston Latin School, Dartmouth College, and the Boston University Law School, Mr. Putnam wrote a column for the Boston Globe newspaper during the 1940's. (His public information officer at HEW says Mr. Putnam still dictates messages to him as a "leg man dictating to a rewrite man.").

In 1948, Mr. Putnam became the 49th member of his family to serve as a state representative. After serving eight years, he became legislative council to U.S. Sen. Leverett Saltonstall. He also served as chief aide to Rep. Joseph W. Martin (R) of Mass.

Chapter 24

PARTY POLITICS

When I emerged from Dartmouth College in 1937, I was innocent of any preference as to party politics. I found much to criticize in both parties.

Yet Franklin D. Roosevelt was at the height of his popularity and his National Youth Administration achieved its purpose of keeping students in college – thereby keeping me off the unemployment rolls. I had reason to be grateful to FDR and the Democratic party that gave us Social Security, an end to the 1929 depression and vast public work projects that were transforming the country.

My earliest memories of partisan politics were Republican. We read the Boston Herald – Republican; not the Post – Democrat; and not the Boston Globe – sort of anemically neutral. I would not have guessed in the 1930s that only the Boston Globe would survive as a major newspaper.

My first lesson in blind partisanship shocked me in 1928 – when I was twelve years old. My parents sat reading the Sunday newspaper in the presence of a couple who were their close friends. The visiting male excused himself to go to the bathroom. My father handed him the front page of the rotogravure section of the Sunday paper, emblazoned with a huge picture of Al Smith, the Democrat candidate for President, with which to wipe himself! I discovered then that Protestants voted for Republicans – Hoover, and Catholics voted for one of their own – Alfred E. Smith, then Governor of New York.

When I made the rounds of newspapers in 1937, seeking a reporter position, my Republican upbringing led me first to the Boston Herald – the leading Republican newspaper in New England. I had my unpleasant interview with editor, Robert Choate. And then I had better luck with the Globe.

During my early years of newspaper work. I felt it my public and professional duty to be politically neutral. I observed the battles, but tried to remain above them. Not with complete success, because my first mentor was Boston City Councillor Clement A. Norton, an ardent New Deal Democrat.

Clem used to spell it out repeatedly: " Boston is more Irish than Dublin, and more Catholic than Rome." And Irish Democrats controlled both the City of Boston and the Commonwealth of Massachusetts. And except for Clem, they were not very supportive of the national Democratic Party and the Roosevelt New Deal.

The most faithful disciple of the New Deal in Boston in the 1930s and 1940s was David K. Niles, executive director of the Ford Hall Forum. The top speakers in the country were invited to Boston for the Sunday evening forums. They received one hour to expound their ideas, and then were exposed to an hour of questions from an intelligent and aggressive audience. I earned my Ph.D. in public affairs at those forums.

My devotion to some of the stalwarts of the Roosevelt administsration was not healthy for my marital relations, especially for my touchy relations with my in-laws – possessive parents of an only child. They were traditional Protestant Republicans. They were appalled that any member of the family would consider favorably anything done by a Democrat.

Fortunately, Navy service in World War 2 gave me some respite from that, and contacts continued with Democratic leaders. Congressman John W. McCormack, on his way to becoming Speaker, showed a fatherly interest in my career, and wrote to me frequently while I was all over the world in active service.

Before and during the war, I used to write a free-wheeling

political column for the Hyde Park Tribune – no pay, but more importantly, no restrictions. At least I was fair enough so that both Senator David I. Walsh, Democrat, and Senator Henry Cabot Lodge, Jr., Republican, were willing to write a guest column for me when I went on vacation.

Only once did I strike a raw nerve. I did not see any good in the Fascist repression of Franco Spain and gasped audibly when the Irish-Catholic-Democrat Commissioner of Education for Massachusetts supported the fascist Generalissimo fervently. I discovered that I was in a small minority in the City of Boston!

I was never sure how my zealous column was being received – except that my in-laws did not like my support of the New Deal and Catholics did not like my criticism of Franco.

When I reached the Massachusetts House of Representatives in 1949 as a new member, it was a great relief to hear Clerk of the House Larry Groves say:

"I love your column in the Tribune. You really tell it like it was – and is!"

Coming from the parliamentarian of the House, famous for his enlightened fairness, those were especially appreciated words. He had to deal with liberal Democrat Tip O'Neill as Speaker from 1948 to 1952, and the very next term with right-wing Republican Charles Gibbons in the Speaker chair. It was the Republican who wound up in deep trouble over his legislative activities.

To run for the " Great and General Court of Massachusetts" (House) in 1948 I had to make a crucial partisan choice. The district of Needham, Dedham and Canton was about four to one Republican . There was no point in swapping my professional neutrality for Democrat; no Democrat could be elected. And I was not comfortable choosing Republican; it seemed to me then the party of the aged and the privileged. (It is still the party of the privileged!).

But it was clear that my name was so well-known from eleven years of by-lines in the Boston Globe that I could probably win the Republican primary, and if I won that, I was sure to be elected. I swallowed my delicate tastes, and plunged into Republican politics.

It was not as bad as I had expected. Whatever was bad, we could change. We could elect leaders who were capable and honest – and even non-Protestant and non-Yankee – and with a cosmopolitan slate we could win some statewide elections. We began doing that with George Fingold, a Jew; Ed Brooke, a black; and John Volpe, an Italian-American Catholic. Fingold was on his way to being Governor when he died suddenly in middle age; Brooke became the only black male ever elected to the United States Senate by popular vote; and Volpe created the Federal interstate highway program under President Eisenhower and later became Governor of Massachusetts.

A political party is only a mechanism to organize people to achieve some public good. Nothing wrong with that! We did much good under the Republican banner from 1948 into the 1960s.

The progress was not without some agonies. My closest ally in the 1948-1956 years was State Senator Sumner G. Whittier of Everett, who devoted his life to becoming Governor. The poet Whittier was somewhere in his ancestry, and his first name was derived from our great Civil War Senator, Charles Sumner of Boston. The original Sumner was responsible for no less than the Emancipation Proclamation, the annexation of Alaska and the United States civil service system.

Sumner Whittier was a marvelous orator, and a principled good fellow, but he had some powerful enemies. Speaker Tip O'Neill nurtured a strong dislike for him. It seemed to be a Protestant-Catholic thing – each was an outstanding disciple of his faith. Tip nicked Sumner at every opportunity with the story of the bag of groceries and the sales tax vote.

The sales tax issue was not Sumner's only Waterloo. We had pounded the Democrats so hard between 1948 and 1952 that we could foretell their sure defeat in the next statewide election.

The Republican nominee for Governor would win, and he would carry his slate with him. But Sumner backed off from the nomination fight.

Fortunately, new leaders were born in that campaign. George Fingold of Concord went on to be a great Attorney General, and would have won a campaign for Governor but for his untimely death.

Edward W. Brooke nearly won a House seat in Roxbury, despite running as a Republican (because of our civil rights record!) in a heavily Democratic district. Governor Volpe in '61 summoned Ed to the State House during the first days of his administration, and I waited in the hall for Brooke to emerge.

"Geez. He wants me to be Secretary of the Governor's Council." Ed was visibly angry. Traditionally, the position always went to a "token" black. Ed had no intention of being anyone's "token black" – he was better educated and a more dynamic personality than the Governor!

"What did you say?"

"No. . . He agreed to come up with something else."

We went back to the State House a week later to find out what better was available. This time when Ed came out of the Governor's Office he looked puzzled:

"What the heck is the Fin Com?"

I could not contain my enthusiasm: "Take it! Take it!... It's the Finance Commission of the City of Boston. You are the watchdog for the State. You can mess into everything!"

Ed had been brought up in Washington, D.C., and had not been exposed to Fin Com headlines all his life, as I had. The agency was an ancient Republican creation, enacted originally to curb the peccidilloes of a rascal Mayor – James Michael Curley.

Mayor Curley knew that a few wealthy Republicans ran their party for their own benefit – and he saw no reason why he could not do the same!

Brooke accepted the position of Chairman of the Boston

Yankee Journal

THE COMMONWEALTH OF MASSACHUSETTS
EXECUTIVE DEPARTMENT
STATE HOUSE, BOSTON

CHRISTIAN A. HERTER
GOVERNOR

July 9, 1953

Honorable Harold Putnam
House Lobby
State House

Dear Harold:

      I have never thanked you for
your good letter of June 23rd in regard to
the Arena. You certainly have been more
than generous on the whole matter and I
am deeply appreciative. I now have my
fingers crossed but hope that the situation
will work out so as to be beneficial to the
community.

      Best, as ever.

Chris

CAH/c

1953 - We preserve the Boston Arena for schoolboy hockey!

Finance Commission and I knew it would be the launching pad for an important political career. Within ten years, Ed became Attorney General, the first black ever elected to statewide office in Massachusetts, and United States Senator, to this day the only black male ever elected to the Senate by popular vote.

It was not painful to be a Republican in the 1950s and 1960s. We offered some fine leaders and accomplished many good things.

We have had worse Presidents than Dwight Eisenhower, and John Volpe and Frank Sargent were good Governors. Senator Leverett Saltonstall and Speaker Joe Martin gave faithful service in Washington.

But I was never a narrow partisan. I always voted against a sale tax and in favor of a graduated income tax (those votes probably cost me a nomination for Congress!). In college I was taught that taxation in an enlightened democracy should be based upon the ability to pay . But those with the ability to pay have never submitted to that fair doctrine. I have concluded in more recent years that that annual vote on a graduated income tax was sneaked onto the agenda of a joint session of the Legislature only to separate the docile sheep from the thoughtful goats. The thoughtful goats were singled out for later slaughter.

I was friendly to labor and social programs – usually Democrat positions. And I liked a young Congressman named John F. Kennedy.

But during the 1950s and the 1960s, the Republican party was a constructive force in Massachusetts, very different from the national Republican party of the 1990s. The Nixon triumph after the death of Jack Kennedy began the different and more bitter and more partisan era. Now it is a fight to the death – and usually over emotional issues that inflame the passions of the less enlightened voters.

Massive campaign funds can mould public opinion to the will of the payor and the incumbent beneficiaries of the corrupt system show no inclination to change it. The United States Senate has become a millionaires' club, supported largely by special interests whose economic and political interests are the same. What chance for a national health insurance system? What chance to protect our natural resources from private depredations? What chance for a simple and fair tax system? Slim chances – under the current election practices.

But history is written in the blood of slim chances. There was only a slim chance that my family could survive and prosper in the Salem Village of 1640. There was only a slim chance that they could build a new nation. There was only a slim chance that they could fight successfully for their freedom from the British Empire.

Lincoln had only a slim chance of preserving the Union. Roosevelt had only a slim chance of saving England in World War 2. As a nation, we had only a slim chance that the Bill of Rights would survive more than two hundred years of constant assaults.

A prophet named Jesus of Nazareth had only a slim chance that his teachings would survive for two thousand years.

I have won some triumphs when I had only a slim chance. I have lost some causes when the slim chances failed. But the troops of good intentions will live to fight another day.

Thank You

I am deeply grateful to the many people who helped me with this project:

To James O. Freedman, the President of Dartmouth College, who found time despite his awesome burdens to read some chapters and to urge this alumnus to write from the heart.

To Michael Contompasis, the current headmaster of my High School, who wrote "good job!" on the chapter on Boston Latin School.

To Barbara Kreiger, professor of creative writing at Dartmouth, whose enthusiasm for the chapter on Sacco and Vanzetti convinced me that I should try some more.

To Diane Raintree, a New York literary agent who advised me to skip a long introduction about my lifelong addiction to biographies, and to cut right to the personal stories.

To my friends at the Kendal retirement home in Hanover, New Hampshire, who read all or some of this work, and who offered helpful comments: Bob and Betty Sincerbeaux, Charles Dudley, Maria Leiper and Joan Williams.

To friends who read the entire manuscript: Jeanne Hoover, member of the Board of Idaho Public Television and wife of Dr. Robert Hoover, the new President of the University of Idaho (our descendants are making them grandparents for the first time and me a great grandparent!); and David W. Fisher, M. Betty Saunders and Richard F. Treadway, all of Vero Beach, Florida.

To the memory of my favorite conservative friend, the late John C. Lee of Vero Beach, Florida, who liked my political stories even though he was really devoted to Ross Perot.

To Jay Evans, the father of kayak racing in America, for checking out my chapter on the 1933 round NewEngland cruise.

To Cindy Lee Cook, who transposed my computer copy into book format at the Hanover Printing Company.

To Ann and Bob Berger, whose generous hospitality has made it possible for me to spend summers in Hanover, New Hampshire, near the throne of learning - Baker Library.

And most of all to my wife, Marlene, for her encouragement and support. She really is a great visual artist, but she has a way with words. If she liked something, it stayed. On the rare occasions when she had reservations, I prudently reconsidered the matter, and usually produced an improved result.

Thanks to all of you— and to the readers who have come this far!

ORDER FORM

BOOKSTORES:

Orders for additional copies of "Yankee Journal" will be shipped on consignment. The suggested retail price of the book is $14. Available to bookstores at the customary trade discount.

Please indicate number of books requested and your address and phone number. Send the order via FAX to 561-231-0195 or by eMail to: hputnam@compuserve.com.

You can write to the author at P. O. Box 3821, Vero Beach, Florida 32964

••

ORDER FORM FOR DIRECT MAIL SHIPMENTS:

Please ship _____ copies of "Yankee Journal" to the address below:

Name: _____

Address: _____

City & State: _____ Zip: _____

Please make the check payable to "The Putnams" and mail it to P. O. Box 3821, Vero Beach, Florida 32964. Enclose $14 per book, plus $2 for postage and handling.